More Praise for
Breakthrough Parenting for Children with Special Needs

"In this exceptional book, author Judy Winter delivers inspiring success stories, specific resources, parent-tested strategies, and validating words that readers can use to help their children achieve better lives. Highly recommended."

—Sam Horn, author, *Tongue Fu!*
and emcee, Maui Writers Conference

"I commend Judy Winter for expressing so honestly the gifts that can be brought about by a commitment to love and defiance against all odds. Her work is one that ought to be taken to heart, regardless of personal situations, as it stands as a tribute to what all people can achieve and what lies at the heart of the human spirit."

—Brooke Ellison, M.A., John F. Kennedy School of Government at Harvard University, author, *Miracles Happen: One Mother, One Daughter, One Journey*

"Inspires the reader to rethink, reframe, and reevaluate their expectations and parenting style. Judy Winter's style is empowering, inspiring, and will help children with special needs everywhere."

—Cherie Carter-Scott, Ph.D., author, *If Life Is a Game, These Are the Rules: Ten Rules for Being Human*

"Judy Winter challenges families and professionals to help children with special needs to reach their full potential through a motivational, how-to approach that works. The book states the importance of focusing on ability, not disability, and provides encouragement through inspiring success stories of parents and caregivers who have been there."

—Susan Titus Osborn, author, *A Special Kind of Love: For Those Who Love Children with Special Needs*

"Judy Winter's book requires me to alter my beliefs and academic content in my instruction to special education teachers and adds another dimension to the preparation of teachers working with special need students."

—Edna Felmlee, instructor,
Special Education Coordinator/
Special Education Internship, Michigan State University

"Vignettes are carefully woven with medical information to make a readable book that every parent of a child with special needs should read. Judy Winter's knowledge and enthusiasm for the topic clearly come through. I strongly recommend this book to all—parents and professionals who work with children with special needs."

—Virginia Simson Nelson, M.D., M.P.H., professor,
Department of Physical Medicine and Rehabilitation,
University of Michigan Medical School

"This book will be a welcomed addition to the libraries of all parents, whether or not they have a child with a disability."

—Linda Wacyk, communications manager,
Michigan Association of School Administrators

"A rare combination of a well-researched, compassionate and no-nonsense, how-to parenting guide for *all* children."

—Clare Leach, licensed professional counselor, Aspen, Colorado

"Ann Frank once said, 'How wonderful it is that nobody need wait a single moment before starting to improve the world.' Judy Winter is doing it eloquently."

—Ronna Robbins, special educator, Detroit Public Schools

"As the mother of two children with special needs I have been inspired by Judy Winter's strength and compassion during a time of great challenges for her family. As a reader, I have been impressed by her ability to tell a story in a way that touches the heart."

—Annie Lewis, Michigan mom of two sons
with Asperger's Syndrome

BREAKTHROUGH PARENTING FOR CHILDREN WITH SPECIAL NEEDS

RAISING THE BAR OF EXPECTATIONS

Judy Winter

JOSSEY-BASS
A Wiley Imprint
www.josseybass.com

Library of Congress Cataloging-in-Publication Data
Winter, Judy, date.
  Breakthrough parenting for children with special needs : raising the bar of expectations / Judy Winter.— 1st ed.
     p. cm.
  Includes bibliographical references and index.
  ISBN-13: 978-0-7879-8081-8 (pbk.)
  ISBN-10: 0-7879-8081-1 (pbk.)
  1. Children with disabilities—Family relationships. 2. Children with disabilities—Care.
  3. Parents of children with disabilities. 4. Parenting. I. Title.
  HQ773.6.W56 2006
  649'.151—dc22   2005034285

Printed in the United States of America
FIRST EDITION

PB Printing 10 9 8 7 6 5 4 3 2 1

CONTENTS

FOREWORD

I first met author Judy Winter when she interviewed me for an article about my experiences with my son who was born with Down syndrome. At that time, she was a successful journalist, loving wife, and full-time mother of two children: a daughter, Jenna, who was thriving in high school, with college in her future, and Eric, her son, who was reaching for his highest potential while living with cerebral palsy.

I was immediately impressed by her passion to use her knowledge and writing talent to support families and professionals who lived and worked in the special needs arena.

As Eric's mother, she had a wonderful understanding of the terrain. Judy networked her way from her own experience to others whose experiences and expertise with special needs she shared through her many articles. Since our first encounter, we formed a friendship from our mutual experiences, passions, and humor. We continued to keep in touch via always-entertaining e-mails.

The e-mail I'll never forget popped up on my screen one day at work. I quickly opened it, knowing that anything from Judy would immediately brighten my day. It was not so that day. The e-mail was short and simply stated that Eric had passed away very suddenly and unexpectedly. What a heavy heart I had. I believe those of us with children with special needs experience parenting in a much more intense way than parents of children with typical needs. I am sure the pain of losing a child is just as strong no matter what a child's needs are. The difference, I believe, is that the void can be cavernous when a parent loses a child with special needs. All those daily activities immediately cease, and you're left alone with time—and time can become your enemy.

Judy embraced that time and used it to keep her relationship with Eric alive, authoring *Breakthrough Parenting for Children with Special Needs: Raising the Bar of Expectations*. She shares from her vast knowledge and personal experience, along with her new unexpected freedom to speak her mind. She is fearless, knowing that she can now openly and honestly share her knowledge, experiences, and views without creating negative consequences to Eric's life.

Nothing can intimidate her now that she lives with the memory of Eric. It frees her to enhance the lives of others through her understanding of these challenges.

Breakthrough Parenting for Children with Special Needs should be provided to parents when any child receives a diagnosis that includes special needs. Those of us who live in that world spend much of our time and money reading multiple books, while attending conferences and classes to teach us how to better meet our child's needs. We try to learn how to maneuver the medical, educational, and community systems, which have many more facets when it comes to providing services for a child with special needs. Judy provides that information in one place, simply and concisely, with compassion and validation.

Breakthrough Parenting for Children with Special Needs offers a more holistic view to professionals who provide services to individuals with special needs. This valuable tool will allow them to step outside their individual discipline and experience the bigger picture of what is going on in the lives of the families they serve, enabling them to better meet each family's individual needs.

Judy addresses the many ins and outs of daily life with a child with special needs. She covers the needs as the child matures.

Chapter titles make the book easy to reference. The support of individual stories makes the information real, personal, and inspirational.

This book is the essential companion for parents and professionals who care for individuals with special needs.

Parenting a child with special needs is unique in that it lasts a lifetime. I am in the early adult years with my own son at this time. I began addressing my concerns for Blair's future when he was still very young. His experiences as a child have contributed greatly to who he has become as an adult.

I wish I had *Breakthrough Parenting for Children with Special Needs* to refer to during his formative years. I had to learn the ways of the Individualized Education Program (IEP) and the rights to an appropriate education. I became a medical expert on my son, often providing important information, bridging various medical specialists and bringing them together.

My husband and I had a vision for Blair's quality of life, and for his future, that we had to share with the professionals who provided services to him. How nice it would have been to refer to *Breakthrough Parenting for Children with Special Needs* during that time in our lives. I am convinced that the journey would have been easier, and I believe we could have addressed some issues more swiftly and more concisely.

Parenting any child is a great responsibility. Helping them to realize their personal strengths and talents, which will bring them to a fulfilled and prosperous life, is challenging and rewarding for all parents. Having special needs added to the equation can sometimes cause a parent to lose focus.

Breakthrough Parenting for Children with Special Needs will assist parents in keeping the necessary perspective while assisting their child with special needs to reach his or her highest potential. This book can provide illuminating, inspiring, and valuable information by reading it cover to cover or by referencing the chapter that will be most meaningful to you at the time.

Either way, you will enjoy and grow from the experience of this wonderful book.

Gail Williamson
Executive Director, Down Syndrome Association of Los Angeles (DSALA)
Mother of Blair Williamson, an actor with Down syndrome
Los Angeles, California

A WORD FROM BROOKE ELLISON

There are very few guarantees in our lives, and it is impossible ever to predict what lies ahead of us. I know this, as I experienced it firsthand when tragedy struck my family and me in 1990. Yet, what keeps us all able to continue to make a difference, irrespective of the challenges we might face, is the very presence of loved ones in our lives. Judy Winter's *Breakthrough Parenting for Children with Special Needs* is a valuable testament to that very idea, and it spoke to so many of the most difficult and most rewarding aspects of my life over the past fifteen years.

When difficulties arise, we are forced to reevaluate both our expectations for our future, as well as the sources of our strength and encouragement. At the same time, there is never a need to underestimate what we all can accomplish together. Through Judy's thoughtful words and insightful examples, she makes clear how the perseverance of any individual can reach heights otherwise unexpected, and it is directly through works like *Breakthrough Parenting for Children with Special Needs* that hope can be restored to people facing the most adverse of circumstances. I commend Judy Winter for expressing so honestly the gifts that can be brought about by a commitment to love and defiance against all odds. Her book is one that ought to be taken to heart, regardless of personal situation, as it stands as a tribute to what all people can achieve and what lies at the heart of the human spirit.

Brooke Ellison
M.A., John F. Kennedy School of Government at Harvard University, 2004
Author, *Miracles Happen: One Mother, One Daughter, One Journey*
Setauket, New York

This book is dedicated to Jenna and Eric Winter—
my greatest life teachers.

In Loving Memory

Eric Richard Winter

Timothy Leach

Max Matthews

Jessica Emery Schneider

Galen Strasburg

Matthew Joseph Thaddeus Stepanek

Christopher Reeve

and

Fred Rogers

Your music lives on . . .

ACKNOWLEDGMENTS

I want to offer my heartfelt thanks to all those families and professionals who shared their inspiring stories, remarkable insight, and unconditional love of children with special needs with me in the pages of *Breakthrough Parenting for Children with Special Needs: Raising the Bar of Expectations*.

Huge thanks to my wonderful agent, Catherine Fowler of the Redwood Agency, and my terrific editor, Alan Rinzler. Your skilled professionalism, mixed with heart, humor, and a real understanding of the value of this project, made the process of turning my dream into reality *a joy*—thank you both for believing in me and this important project right from the start. You have helped create something truly special!

Many thanks to all the great people at Jossey-Bass responsible for overseeing the production and marketing of *Breakthrough Parenting for Children with Special Needs: Raising the Bar of Expectations*, especially Catherine Craddock, Paul Foster, Susan Geraghty, Paula Goldstein, Carol Hartland, Marcy Marsh, Seth Schwartz, Patrick Seitz, Karen Warner, and Jennifer Wenzel. Thank you all for your individual expertise, hard work, valuable suggestions, and great enthusiasm for this wonderful project—and thanks for putting Eric's great face on the book's cover, where he belongs!

Special thanks to Dana Reeve, chairperson of the Christopher Reeve Foundation; Timothy Shriver, Ph.D., chairman of Special Olympics; and Diane Bubel, executive director of the Bubel/Aiken

Foundation for their support of this amazing project—and for the valuable work they do each day on behalf of those with special needs worldwide. You are an inspiration.

Thanks to all the skilled professionals with great heart who looked beyond Eric's wheelchair to help a bright, talented, eager, and engaging young child achieve his fondest dreams—and who lost their hearts in the process, especially, Andrea Benyovszky and the wonderful Conductive Learning Center staff, Cindy Lu Edgerton, LaVelle Gipson-Tansil, Moe Hill, Kim Hills, Ellen McCreedy, Alison Meinke, Jaime Merritt, Erin Nicholas, and Brenda Lou Turner. You have all become family.

Special thanks to Dr. Mark Takagishi, Jan Schwartz, R.N., and the great Lansing Pediatrics staff—who *almost* made it fun to go the doctor.

To Eric's many wonderful friends, especially his best friends, Sam Hadar and Kelly Jameson, who taught us all the true meaning of *inclusion* and friendship.

To all those families who work incredibly hard each and every day to make their children's lives the best they can be—I salute you.

Thanks to siblings everywhere for all the sacrifices you make each day so that your brothers and sisters can live out their dreams, too—you are my heroes.

To my spiritual guide, mentor, and dear friend, the Reverend Rosemary Chaffee, who has helped me stand tall during some pretty tough life storms—you are a treasure.

To Kate, Stacy, and John at McNenly Group for your marketing genius.

To everyone at the Maui Writers Conference—it's paradise and my lucky charm.

To the magnificent blue heron that *always* appears in my backyard when I most need to be inspired—and feel my son's presence.

To all of my wonderfully talented, smart, funny, and supportive women friends, who get better with age, especially Jane Aldrich, Jeanie Croope, Sharon Emery, Clare Leach, Ronna Robbins, Susan

Rochau, Holly Sasso, Linda Wacyk, and Gail Williamson. I love you guys—thanks for keeping me humble and making me laugh.

To Grandma Mary, whose unconditional love of her grandson inspired us all.

To my family, especially my husband, Dick, a great partner and wonderful dad. Where would I have been without all those short convertible escapes—and your financial support, computer savvy, and willingness to take on cooking duties as I took on the awesome challenge of trying to do Eric's legacy justice? Much love and thanks.

My deepest thanks go to my incredible kids, Jenna and Eric Winter, who taught me to grant the sacred role of parenting the full respect and attention it deserves. You have both made me so proud and have helped me achieve more than I thought possible. I love you with all my heart and soul, *forever!*

Finally, thanks to God, who in his own time and way *always* comes through . . .

JENNA'S POEM

In My Dreams (Eric)

Jenna Marie Winter

In my dreams, I saw my brother walk.
He chased me around the house,
His cerebral palsy gone.
He talked to me about the things we've missed
Over the years.
It was nice to hear his voice,
His real voice,
For the first time,
And we conversed till midnight.
He yawned and told me to take him outside,
Down to the pond.
We caught frogs by flashlight,
But they wiggled out of his small, inexperienced hands.
He giggled with delight,
Told me that he liked the way that they felt.
I gave him a ride back up to the house,
His sleepy head bobbing up and down
On my shoulder.
I slipped him into bed,
Covered his brand new body,
His brand new strength.
As I looked down at him,
He opened his eyes,
And he smiled up at me.
I smiled back tears
That threatened to fall as,
Unbroken,
He told me that he loved me.

Written at age fourteen by Eric Winter's incredible big sister
Third-place award, National Society of
Arts and Letters Poetry Contest 2000

BREAKTHROUGH PARENTING FOR CHILDREN WITH SPECIAL NEEDS

INTRODUCTION: RAISING THE BAR OF EXPECTATIONS FOR CHILDREN WITH SPECIAL NEEDS

Anyone who does anything to help a child in this life is a hero to me.

—Fred Rogers

Welcome to *Breakthrough Parenting for Children with Special Needs*.

If you've been searching for an empowering, motivational, and user-friendly resource to help you parent a child with special needs—you've just found it.

Whether your child received his or her special needs diagnosis at birth or at some other point during childhood, teen, or young-adult years, *Breakthrough Parenting for Children with Special Needs: Raising the Bar of Expectations* was written for you.

A New Way of Looking at Your Situation

This book challenges parents and professionals to maximize the potential of children and young adults with special needs by using a motivational, how-to approach that *gets results*. It includes parent-tested strategies, valuable resources, and inspiring success stories to help provide families and professionals with renewed hope for creating better lives and greater independence for millions of children with special needs.

Breakthrough Parenting for Children with Special Needs is not about *fixing* children with special needs; it's about changing the way in which families, professionals, and society *view* and *interact* with these children. That powerful shift in thinking helps make this book special.

This book is about personal empowerment and making the kind of changes that lead to better lives for all kids no matter what role you play on a special needs team. It's about taking individual responsibility for your impact on a child.

Professionals working with the special needs population may gain greater sensitivity about the challenges facing these families—and further insight into their demanding lives.

My hope is that this book will challenge all professionals to reexamine how they interact with families. My suggestion is that they work harder to look beyond disability and focus on a child's value, potential, and abilities, while sharing valuable resources and expertise with the families they serve.

How This Book Works

This book is filled with inspiring personal success stories from families who have triumphed over a wide range of special needs, including cerebral palsy, multiple sclerosis, Down syndrome, autism, and hearing and sight impairments. These stories will energize and motivate you, make you stand up and cheer—and maybe even move you to tears.

This book recognizes the valuable role of siblings.

Readers will benefit from The Special Needs Bill of Rights for Children, Parents, Siblings, and Professionals, which offer the people most affected by the demands of special needs the permission to embrace their valuable roles. This family-friendly resource also allows readers to quickly access valuable resources and special tips for success at the end of each chapter.

From chapter to chapter, you will learn from the experts—the families facing special needs parenting challenges day in–day out,

24/7, 52 weeks a year, including weekends, holidays, and Christmas—*for life*.

This book is a comprehensive, valuable, and timeless resource guide for all parents and professionals, which will help them better understand the value and potential of children and young adults with special needs, as well as their siblings. All challenges are viewed as having equal importance.

Although not every special needs diagnosis or parenting situation is directly identified in this book (you wouldn't be able to lift it!), all special needs challenges are considered important—whether spoken or unspoken.

The book's solid focus on parent empowerment and making decisions that help all children succeed makes *Breakthrough Parenting for Children with Special Needs* of value for anyone who cares about helping children live more fulfilling lives, whether they face physical, behavioral, emotional, medical, or developmental challenges.

Who Am I to Write This Book?

Within each chapter, you will find parent-tested strategies from a mom with more than a decade of special needs parenting experience. Me. For nearly thirteen years, I successfully parented a child with cerebral palsy, a wheelchair user with limited speech and few motor skills.

My son passed away suddenly in 2003 at age twelve.

Parenting Eric was the most difficult and most rewarding thing I have ever done in my life. This book is a tribute to my son's remarkable life and to his many impressive achievements—some of which I will share with you in these pages.

I wrote this book for Eric so we could help change other children's lives.

This resource will encourage you to reach for the parenting stars, while reminding you of the need to face and address some critical facts about your child's diagnosis. You will be challenged to change your focus from what you *can't* change to what you *can* change.

Empowered parents are the key to creating better lives for *all* children, including those with special needs. You are the *real* experts regarding your child. This book recognizes and validates that important fact, while challenging you to up your parenting game.

This guide challenges the perception that having a child with special needs is a fate worse than death. It will encourage parents to celebrate and value their children's existence as a remarkable parenting gift.

Three Things I Already Know About You

Before we get started, allow me to share three things I know for sure—and I didn't learn them in kindergarten, college, or the workplace!

- *If you are just starting out on this often-unpredictable and emotional parenting road, I have a pretty good idea about where you are.* You're overwhelmed, scared, confused, angry at yourself, your child, the world, or God. You're trying to be hopeful and wanting more for your child, but you're afraid to dream.

- *I've got a pretty clear idea about where you're headed and what awaits you when you get there.* You'll find societal roadblocks, accessibility challenges, outdated stereotypes, funding and political debates, and professional arrogance, which will test your creativity, patience, endurance, sanity, blood pressure, and anger management skills. Fortunately, there is an ongoing disability rights movement that helps fuel all of these much-needed societal changes.

- *I'm darn sure that you can survive—and even thrive—in your new parenting role.* You'll need to do a lot of hard work, have a positive attitude, and get the right kind of parenting support. I am living proof that it can be done. If I can take on this unexpected role and thrive, so can you!

Why Do I Believe All This When I've Never Met You or Your Child?

Because I was where you are now, and I know where you are headed. I have walked many challenging miles in your parenting shoes. I was the same unsure-but-hopeful, loving, dedicated parent of a child with special needs, hungry for the validation, support, and positive examples of other families. I went searching for good resources and came up empty-handed, discouraged, and outraged. More than once, the frustrations of navigating public education tempted me to home school my child.

I was that parent who didn't know which way to turn next, who had to try to figure it all out by herself, without the benefit of good resources like this one. (They didn't exist when my son was born.) But I refused to *ever* give up on my child.

My special needs parenting demands caused me to fall to my knees more than once, while allowing me to become a much better human being than I ever imagined possible. The demands of special needs challenged me to the limits of human endurance—and helped me realize my most heartfelt life dreams, too.

It was the intensity of my own parenting challenges that made me decide to write this book. I want to reach out to those families who are coming behind me. I want them to have something to hold on to—tightly and securely—as they walk what can be at best an uncertain parenting path.

Because of Eric's needs, I became a more educated and empowered parent. I learned how to love unconditionally and redefine perfection and disability. I now understand fully the sacred and tremendous responsibility of being a child's parent.

Today I focus on possibilities and solutions, not on problems or dismal statistics. I learned to celebrate my son's *imperfection* as a blessing. Parenting Eric was the most life-changing and demanding experience of my life. I would do it again in a heartbeat.

How to Use This Book

When I first began this uncertain and challenging journey, I was a novice. But I became a master at successfully addressing my son's significant needs so he could have a better life. Far too many families are living lives of desperation and hopelessness. This is an injustice, unworthy of our children, and I want to change it, with your help—and this book!

I will be asking you to step up to the parenting plate big time! Raising children with special needs is not for the squeamish, the complainers, the unforgiving, the overachievers, or the control freaks—unless they want to change. You need to have a *Rocky-like* and *Mother-Teresa-like* mentality, which you can develop by *using this book*.

You must be willing to embrace change without moaning and groaning too loudly, if you are going to be able to effectively help your children recognize their full potential in a world that often devalues them, then looks the other way.

Offering your children every opportunity to have the life they deserve demands pit-bull determination. But throughout the pages of this book, I will walk you through every step of the way. I will support and challenge you, provide friendship and understanding, and share your tears—and I'll celebrate with you, too.

I will walk you through some of the most difficult transitions, stages, and unnerving meetings, by providing you with the information and resources required to help you become an *increasingly empowered parent*. (Note that I've redefined the term *IEP*.)

Finally, I will challenge you to get back into the parenting ring when you've been delivered a knockout punch from which you are certain you can never recover.

I *know* you can—I've been there. Not a single day goes by when I don't miss Eric deeply. I will never, *ever* forget the impact he had and continues to have on my life—and on my work. He taught me so many profound lessons that continue today.

How did I reach such acceptance and love for my son? First, I had to come to terms with my new parenting role by doing necessary grief work. I had to let go of old parenting dreams to make room for the new. I made tough personal choices that led to personal empowerment. I refused to embrace a life of despair. I became outraged by all the societal intolerance and discrimination that I witnessed. And I was determined to use that raw energy to create positive social change. I allowed myself to be guided by strong personal faith and the saving grace of humor.

But my most important life decision was choosing to view my son as a child first, not as a disability. That decision freed me to raise him as a regular kid, with special challenges, instead of as a *handicapped* child. My attitude shifted from grieving his disability to celebrating one child's amazing abilities. That difference was huge.

I refused to *ever* give up on my dreams—or on my son.

Before Eric's death in 2003, he was fully included in the sixth grade in his neighborhood school, something I had been told would never happen. He had claimed his place on the school honor roll and had appeared in full-page color in *Parents* magazine, part of a pictorial of confident children with special needs from across the country.

Near the end of his life, Eric was composing music during his weekly music therapy classes. I could not have envisioned this reality when he was first born. Having special needs was just a small part of who my son was.

When I first began this journey, my perception of my new role as the parent of a child with a disability was clouded over by fear and an overwhelming sense of inadequacy. Both were fed by a lack of upbeat, motivational parenting resources and deeply ingrained societal stereotypes that devalued my son.

Rigid societal systems, public policies, and discrimination are not easy to rise above, nor are personal exhaustion, the loss of parenting dreams, and the threat of financial ruin. The trick is to learn how to move forward and make good decisions, no matter what challenges you face each day. It *is* possible.

After my son's birth, I was frustrated because all the best parenting magazines appeared to totally ignore families facing special needs. I went searching in vain for upbeat, motivational resources to help me parent my son and came up empty-handed. I remember thinking that it should not be this difficult to raise *any* child.

In the months following my son's birth, I dreamed of writing a motivational book to help parents and professionals do a better job of raising children with special needs. It would be attractive, upbeat, and inspiring, filled with good information and great resources. It would provide the emotional support that many parents need just to get out of bed in the morning. It would make us laugh at the absurdity of our daily demands.

For thirteen years, I lived out the pages of that book. The book that is now in your hands is the result of my amazing journey. I wrote it so you and your child could have better lives. It fulfills a big promise that I made to my incredible son. I wish he were here to see it . . .

Avoiding Quick and Easy Fixes

Breakthrough Parenting for Children with Special Needs: Raising the Bar of Expectations doesn't promise you magical parenting solutions or quick fixes. There are none.

Raising children with special needs to achieve their full potential is hard work. The information here will not cure a child's special needs, nor should it be used as a substitute for medical treatment. Children may still require the use of a wheelchair or other adaptive equipment, tutoring services, and intensive therapy, including drugs or outside placement. Parents may struggle with sleep deprivation for years. Marriages may still end.

What *will* change is how parents and professionals view their situations and how they choose to address their challenges in increasingly empowered ways. That gives me hope for the future of all children with special needs.

You may decide to read this book from cover to cover, or you may find it helpful to jump from chapter to chapter. Do what works best for you. What matters most is that you use it!

To recognize the increasingly rich and diverse definition of the term *family*, whenever *parent* is used, it means the adult legally responsible for a child's daily care, well-being, and legal guardianship.

The term *parent* recognizes, validates, and honors all adults raising children with special needs—whether that role falls to the birth, adoptive, foster, or single parent or to grandparents who have unselfishly given up their own retirement years to take care of a child. All adults who take great care of our kids are heroes in my book.

Is This Book for You?

Before continuing on, please answer the following questions:

- Are you tired of searching for the encouragement, understanding, and validation that you deserve in your role as a parent or as a professional?
- Are you willing to stop complaining about your role and instead start embracing tough personal change to become a more dynamic and empowered parent or professional?
- Are you willing to work harder than you have ever worked in your life to ensure that a child's future (and your own) is the best it can be?
- Are you willing to stand up for a child and for that child's future?

If you answered yes to these important questions, then this book is for you! It's time now to get into the best parenting shape of your life. You have nothing to gain but a brighter future—for you, and for your child.

The choice is yours.

Now let's turn to Chapter One and see how you can embrace some brand-new parenting dreams—and address Asperger's Syndrome. You are beginning a challenging and rewarding journey that leads to parenting empowerment. Welcome aboard!

PART ONE

WELCOME TO *BREAKTHROUGH PARENTING FOR CHILDREN WITH SPECIAL NEEDS*

JUDY WINTER'S
SPECIAL NEEDS BILL OF RIGHTS FOR CHILDREN AND YOUNG ADULTS

You have the right to

- Be treated with dignity and respect
- Celebrate your birth
- Grieve the loss of a life without special needs
- Move about freely in society
- Be seen as a person first, not as a disability
- Obtain a good education, including higher education
- Pursue your dreams, too
- Be proud of your achievements
- Live a full and productive life
- Be included in important decisions made about your life
- Ask tough questions, including *Why?*

1

THE PERFECT-BABY DREAM

Some men see things as they are and ask why. Others dream things that never were and ask why not.

—George Bernard Shaw

Welcome to Chapter One: The Perfect-Baby Dream.

You are beginning an amazing journey filled with unexpected challenges and incredible rewards—gifts you cannot begin to understand when you first start walking down this demanding road. Parenting a child with special needs will be the greatest challenge of your life, and if you make good choices, it may also prove one of the most rewarding.

Unfortunately, too many people feel sorry for these families and believe their children lack value or need to be *fixed*. Prevalent and outdated stereotypes of special needs families are fueled in part by ignorance, and in part by society's obsession with human perfection and physical beauty, including for children. You can help change those stereotypes.

This chapter will challenge you to see your child's life as worth celebrating, while motivating you to make more dynamic parenting choices. You will learn that accepting and valuing children with special needs is the first step toward becoming a healthier special needs family and that a combination of hard work, a family's determination, early intervention, and unconditional love will lead to brighter futures for most children, regardless of their diagnosis.

Beginning with this chapter, you will benefit from the guidance of those who have walked in your shoes. By sharing their stories, these experienced parents will help you learn how to embrace your challenging new role. They have been where you are right now, and they know what lies ahead. Their words will inspire, motivate, and energize you and give you hope.

The information included in this chapter and others won't change the reality of your child's special needs diagnosis. But it may help change how you perceive and respond to those needs. That's a powerful shift in thinking.

So let's begin this journey together with a story from a real-life expert—the mother of two children with Asperger's Syndrome.

A SUCCESS STORY

Annie Lewis's spirit of adventure began long before she became the mother of two children with Asperger's Syndrome, a role that today often defines her.

The forty-eight-year-old mom was a ski patroller in Aspen, Colorado, a millionaire's nurse, a chef in a five-star restaurant, and Cher's maid. Amid the beauty and pristine air of the Colorado Rocky Mountains, Lewis also trained relentlessly, pursuing her dream of biking across China and Europe with her husband, Mark Pullano.

As an athlete, she was used to pushing herself to the limits of physical and mental endurance. But Annie Lewis couldn't train hard enough for autism.

"Autism is a broad spectrum, neurological disorder," Lewis, a nurse, explains. "That means people with autism vary in their abilities and exhibit an entire range of intelligence, responsiveness, and social functioning, from mild to severe."

To the layperson, that means everything from the familiar stereotype of someone rocking in the corners, seemingly oblivious to the world around them, to a child who bites classmates and is obsessed with trains. It can also mean someone with the ability to work with and influence millions of people through impressive life achievements.

Lewis's sons both have Asperger's Syndrome (AS), a form of autism found in high-functioning children and adults, who exhibit some but not all tendencies of autism. Her thirteen-year-old son, Gregg, was diagnosed with Asperger's Syndrome at age four. His eleven-year-old brother, Max, was diagnosed with AS when he was six years old.

Lewis says that all individuals with autism exhibit three key tendencies: impaired socialization, impaired verbal or nonverbal communication, and restricted and repetitive patterns of behavior. "One of best definitions of autism I have ever read is morbid self-interest," she adds. "The one trait universal to all people with autism is the inability to ever see the point of view of another person."

The incidence of autism in the general population is 0.2 percent, but Lewis says the risk of having a second or additional child with autism jumps to nearly 10 to 20 percent. Some have argued that environmental factors play a role in autism. Lewis believes the cause is solely genetic.

One thing she knows for certain, parenting two sons with AS is the toughest life challenge she's ever faced. She's handled it successfully for more than a decade.

Taking Charge of Autism

According to Kathy Johnson, associate director of the Autism Society of Michigan , autism is a neurological disorder that impairs both socialization and communication. Autism is the most common of a spectrum of disorders, including Asperger's Syndrome, with challenges ranging from mild to severe.

Johnson says that the lifelong disability usually appears during the first thirty months of a child's life and occurs in 1 out of every

166 births. It is four times more common in males than females and there is no cure. But early diagnosis and aggressive intervention can help children with autism lead more productive lives.

The number of cases of autism has skyrocketed in recent years, but its cause remains a mystery. Unlike children with lower-functioning autism, children with Asperger's Syndrome have communication and language skills and normal IQs; some are highly intelligent, even gifted.

They may do well in school academically and have successful careers. Many people with AS may be considered odd or eccentric, especially because of their challenged social skills, including the avoidance of prolonged eye contact and difficulty developing meaningful peer relationships.

Johnson says that some people now believe that some of the most brilliant and accomplished individuals in history, including Albert Einstein and Thomas Jefferson, may have had undiagnosed AS.

People with autism have difficulty seeing connections between life events. "It's as if everything that happens to them in life is new," Annie Lewis explains. To help others better understand this autistic tendency, Lewis likes to tell a story:

"If you were to tell a child with autism or Asperger's Syndrome to go knock on the neighbor's door, they would probably understand that request. But they might stand there all day knocking on the neighbor's door, waiting for what's going to happen next," she says. "They don't understand they are waiting for someone to answer the door."

As a nurse, Lewis knew something was wrong before her first-born son was diagnosed with AS at age four. Gregg exhibited many familiar autistic tendencies. His social challenges made it tough for him to play with other kids or form lasting friendships. He had an inability to tolerate the kind of excessive noise and unstructured play that is common during recess and riding the school bus, and he showed a lack of empathy for the feelings of others.

Gregg began hitting and biting classmates at his preschool, throwing tempter tantrums, grabbing toys away from his classmates

as if they didn't exist. He lacked the ability to focus in group settings. The staff worked hard to find an intervention that worked,
but when their efforts failed, Gregg was asked to leave the school.
His mother calls it the worst day of her life.

But she refused to give up on her son and for the next five
months searched for elusive answers about Gregg's challenging
behavior. "When I first started reading about Asperger's Syndrome,"
Lewis explains, "Gregg was right there on the page."

Armed with hope for a firm diagnosis, and what Lewis calls "the
Michael Jordan of preschool teachers," she was successful in returning Gregg to his preschool. The staff agreed to take him back after
he'd had a few months of growth and development. Upon his
return, the school had a system in place to deal with him one on
one. "It was part of thoughtful planning, overseen by a brilliant and
compassionate school director," Lewis says. "We were very, very
lucky."

But it was more than just luck. The crucial decision that Gregg's
mother made to educate herself about his special needs early on,
combined with her determination to help Gregg return to the only
preschool that would accept him, has made a big difference in his
life. "Addressing your child's needs early can mean the difference
between having a functional or nonfunctional child with autism,"
Lewis stresses.

When asked to rate the effort that went into this stage of the
parenting game on a scale of 1 to 10 (10 being toughest), Lewis calls
it a 55. "It was 24/7," she explains. "Gregg was out of school for five
months and I cried nonstop."

Lewis also read voraciously, using her career as a nurse to access
the National Library of Medicine (NLM) online services. She read
every article about autism written in 1994. "We were still in the
dark ages about autism and what I read frightened me," Lewis
explains. She wanted something better for her son. "I never
believed we would not be successful," she says.

Lewis understands well the importance of aggressively addressing the toddler and preschool years, when a child's brain is still

developing. Research now indicates that many children with autism have better outcomes if they receive solid intervention during those critical developmental years. More about early intervention in Chapter Four.

Still, many of these children are not correctly diagnosed until they are older, often due to concerns about labeling or misdiagnosis because of a lack of universal availability of routine screening tools. Gregg wasn't officially diagnosed with autism until he was age four.

According to a report by the *American Academy of Neurology and the Child Neurology Society* (www.aan.com/professionals), the average age of diagnosis of autism is age six, even though most parents felt something was wrong by age eighteen months and had sought out medical attention by age two.

That angers Lewis. "We have got to do a better job of diagnosing these children early," she stresses. "The brain is like a sponge during those early years," Lewis says of this important focus. "It's the difference between writing in sand at age two and chipping away at granite at age ten."

Lewis had to fight her insurance company to have Gregg tested. "They didn't know autism is a neurological disorder," she says with disbelief. "They kept telling me he needed mental health care, not a neurologist. It took months of begging and phone calls for me to get the authorization necessary for the comprehensive testing I knew my son needed, testing that is today a standard of care."

Thanks to his family's persistence, Gregg is now an eighth grader in a regular classroom, with the support of a skilled paraprofessional that Lewis calls "her angel." "Jane understands Gregg well," Lewis says. "She helps him see the connections between things that are happening in his school day and make sense of it."

Children with autism are often unfairly viewed by society as being unruly children, the result of nothing more than bad parenting or lack of discipline. Nothing could be further from the truth. Preparation time and familiar routines are important to children with AS. "We are asking them to come out of their autistic worlds, to be fully present in our world and do things our way," Lewis adds. "It is an incredibly hard thing for them to do."

At age thirteen, Gregg still exhibits some classic autistic traits, including sensitivity to external stimuli. "He doesn't do well with unstructured chaos," Lewis says. That includes noise in the school hallways and riding the bus. But Gregg carries an A average in most of his classes. Lewis now schedules two hours after school each day to allow her son to be totally absorbed in his love of trains. "Gregg needs to spend time in his autistic world," she explains.

As Lewis struggled to bike up a steep mountain incline years ago, a friend warned that the greatest challenge facing her was mental not physical. When her second son, Max, was also diagnosed in 1999 at age six with AS, obsessive-compulsive disorder (OCD), and an IQ placing him in the top 1 percent of the population, Lewis finally understood the true power of that message:

A tough mental attitude gives you an edge in surviving life's tough challenges.

Lewis credits her son's preschool teacher for voicing concern when, at age five, Max had difficulty interacting with other kids, something his mother had never witnessed. Lewis immediately had him tested, and at age six, he was also diagnosed with AS. "Max was so different from Gregg. He was so smart and verbal and high functioning. It never occurred to me that he might also have AS."

Max's multiple special needs diagnosis presents its own challenges. "I've learned that every child is different," she stresses. "What is right for one child may not be right for another, even in the same family. There is no magic formula for meeting the challenges of autism."

Today Max is in the sixth grade with the same teacher his brother once had. "She *gets* him," Lewis says of this important educational partnership.

Lewis has chosen to respond to special needs parenting in the same way she's faced other life adventures—with cutting wit, solid focus, and a winning attitude. Her life hasn't been free of heartache, and Lewis knows another tough parenting demand is always just around the corner.

For the sake of her sons, she works hard to keep her role in perspective and finds solace in simple things like humor and gratitude. "I've learned how to just be grateful for something as simple as a hot cup of morning tea and time alone to drink it."

It's an important lesson for all parents.

LETTING GO OF THE PERFECT-BABY DREAM

One of the most important decisions that Lewis and other successful parents of children with special needs make is to view their children as *children first*, not as disabilities. With perfect-baby images assaulting us at every diaper change, that's no easy task. Popular mainstream parenting magazines help fuel the perfect-baby dream with their glossy publications featuring picture-perfect cover kids.

Care to guess if any of these magazines have included a child with Down syndrome on its cover? Or whether a child using a wheelchair has appeared in a photo essay for magical birthday parties, next to the advertising for premium cotton pajamas?

It will happen when enough adults advocate for societal change that celebrates diversity and redefines our definition of a child's beauty. That means you!

Annie Lewis raised $11,000 for an accessible playground in her neighborhood, spent fourteen days camping outside a Krispy Kreme Donuts shop to create greater awareness of Asperger's Syndrome, and has future plans of group-home ownership! More about advocacy in Chapter Six.

What will your parenting legacy be?

Debunking Perfect-Parenting Mythology

Every year, businesses spend millions of dollars marketing perfect-baby images that do little to prepare anyone for the reality of parenting. We love talking about babies using high-pitched baby

ANNIE LEWIS'S TIPS

Asperger's Syndrome

Having been through the experience of parenting two sons with special needs, Annie Lewis offers five key strategies for success with Asperger's Syndrome:

- *Stay focused on your child.* "Everything in my life has changed, but not my solid focus on and love for my kids."

- *Address the child's needs early in life.* "Spending even ten minutes with your child at age three or four to impact brain development can equal a month or more of working with that child at age ten. It's like working with wet cement versus drilling away at granite. You cannot get those developmental years back."

- *Know when to ask for help.* "I am a strong person who can handle anything I set my mind to. But no matter how strong you are, there are times when you need to ask for help—and 98 percent of the time, people are just waiting for you to ask."

- *Find a way around the obstacles presented, whatever it takes.* "Never give up. There is *always* a way to get around life's obstacles to meet your child's challenges."

- *Put your child's diagnosis in perspective.* "I've learned just to be grateful for all that we have. There are so many people worse off than we are. Addressing autism is tough, but we can handle it. We're educated and we have jobs and health insurance. Some families don't have any of these things."

voices. We laugh just thinking about nuzzling silky baby hair, savoring sweet baby smells, and buying cute little yellow rubber duckies that float in the tub.

But we don't dare talk about smelly diapers that make you gag, sleep deprivation, postpartum depression, kids using wheelchairs or leg braces, surgeries for babies born with heart conditions or other health challenges. We can't imagine that one day our child might be included in the alarming statistics for mental illness, teen depression, suicide, or drug abuse.

We don't prepare families for the heartbreaking reality that despite their best efforts and most heartfelt prayers, their seriously challenged children may die.

When we first become parents, most of us are incredibly naive. Parenting is a tremendous responsibility, especially if your child has special needs. Raising our children to have brighter futures means that families must first let go of their perfect-baby dreams. It is the toughest parenting role that anyone will ever undertake, and one of the most rewarding.

It deserves our full commitment and respect.

Accepting Your Child

Having a child with special needs *demands* that you take your parenting role seriously and become increasingly less selfish. Or pay the steep price.

Regardless of what messages society constantly feeds us, perfect families don't exist. Most children and their parents face challenges during the child's developmental years. Every one of these children, including those with special needs, has value. Understanding that value is the beginning of accepting your child and becoming an increasingly empowered parent.

Repeat after me: my child is worthy of my time, efforts, patience, respect, and love, no matter what challenges he (or she) may face in this life!

To all those creative marketing geniuses and magazine editors who virtually ignore the needs of millions of gutsy families who are looking to create better lives for children with special needs, we boldly wave our disposable income in the competitive retail air and shout, "Shame on you!"

To the parents of these children, I say, "Demand better!"

FORGING NEW PARENTING DREAMS

At some point on this special needs journey, most parents find themselves yearning for the freedom to again pursue romantic interludes and exciting careers, read current magazines cover to cover—and enjoy a full night's sleep.

It's the lack of personal freedom that comes with this demanding new role that makes adjusting to special needs especially tough. Your life has been forever changed, often in unexpected and dramatic ways. No wonder it's so easy to lose your bearings and focus on the negative and even think about giving up on your child. I challenge you to make better choices.

You will not adjust to this new parenting reality overnight. Forging new parenting dreams and becoming a confident parent of a child with special needs take time, tears, teamwork, a deep commitment to your child, and an abundance of unconditional love and patience. You are in this for the long haul.

The parenting rewards you desire come in stages and may not be fully realized until your child is older, especially if your child is facing a particularly challenging diagnosis. No one can predict with certainty what your child's future outcome will be, not even professionals with the most impressive credentials. Still, the choices you make today may well help determine how bright that future is for your entire family.

Every single moment spent with your child matters—even if the only thing you have the energy to do that day is tell your children that you love them. This helps boost your children's self-esteem and sense of value, which will serve them well on the most challenging days.

Speaking from Experience

I was fortunate to parent a child with cerebral palsy for nearly thirteen years. Eric was a wheelchair user with limited speech and mobility. Together we survived many tough life challenges. Despite his many challenges my son was one of the brightest, most joyful, and determined spirits I have ever known.

Being Eric and Jenna's mom has been the most humbling and rewarding experience of my life.

The early years of my son's life were rough. As his parents, we were fed many negatives regarding Eric's life and future, or lack thereof. We were told that he would never achieve much in life and would probably never progress beyond the developmental age of six months.

Professionals kept waiting for him to stop developing, but he never did. Why? Because from the moment of his birth, we chose to raise him as loved and valued. We gave him every opportunity to thrive and sought out important programs that nurtured his potential and celebrated his value, not those prejudging his worth. We treated him like the valued member of our family that he was, just like his sister.

Eric knew he was loved and it served him well. At the end of his life, our son was fully included in his neighborhood school. He had many friends and had begun composing music. He wanted to go to college and study music, a dream we planned to fully support. Eric's life was filled with challenges. Because we chose to roll up our parenting sleeves right from the start, it was also full of dreams and opportunities and great joy.

We accepted and addressed the needs of Eric's disability, but we also focused on nurturing his entire being. That big shift in thinking equaled positive results. It was hard work each and every day of his life, but our parenting efforts were rewarded over and over again with the love and remarkable achievements of an enchanting young child adored by many. Today our son's lessons live on in the lives of many.

I *know* that helping your children have better lives is worth every ounce of your energy, sweat, and tears—no matter how painstaking or small those gains may seem at first. If given the parenting opportunity, I would do it all over again. That's how deeply my son, and daughter, changed my life.

Celebrate your child's life, no matter how rough the start. You are building the foundation of his future life success. Build it rock solid and cement it with love, acceptance, and possibilities. Then be patient with your child—and yourself—as you both work toward achieving your life goals, wherever those dreams may take you.

Recognizing Your Child's Value

When expectant parents are asked whether or not they want a baby boy or a baby girl, they often recite a familiar response: "We don't care, as long as it's healthy." I'm still amazed at how many people said this to me in front of my son! After the delivery, another simplistic statement helps many parents believe they've escaped infant imperfection:

Our baby has ten fingers and ten toes!

I can hear a loud collective sigh of relief from parents counting baby digits across the planet. Guess what? Most children with special needs have ten fingers and ten toes, too! Kind of tosses that perfect-newborn test right out of the incubator, doesn't it?

We are a nation obsessed with physical beauty and perfection. The idea that we could give birth to anything less than a perfect child is too frightening to even consider, so we don't prepare families for the possibility. No wonder when it happens so many parents feel overwhelmed and cheated, as if they have somehow failed at the perfect-baby game.

Celebrating your child's value, while those around you are loudly citing human imperfection and scary statistics, is the beginning of *acceptance*. Stop listening to all the negatives being spouted about your child.

Take in important facts, not uninformed opinions or worst-case scenarios. You need good information, including an accurate diagnosis, to help your child achieve the kind of life success that rarely can be predetermined at the moment of birth. All the negative garbage will only weigh you down. Throw it out!

No child's life should be considered less valuable because they have special needs. It is only one part of who they are and who they may become with your love and support. Work hard to connect with your child in one positive way every single day. It's worth it. *They* are worth it.

CONFRONTING SPECIAL NEEDS PARENTING MYTHS

Allow me to dash a couple of other pervasive myths about children and special needs.

Myth Number One: If your child enters the world without challenges, your family has escaped the dreaded curse of special needs parenting.

Have you seen children in your neighborhood riding bikes or scooters without wearing helmets? Do you know kids who are engaging in risky behaviors like snowboarding, skateboarding, or playing chicken with cars in heavy traffic—a game they usually lose? Do your children play hockey or football or drive recklessly or abuse alcohol and other drugs? All of these behaviors may increase the risk of having special needs, especially if your child suffers a brain injury. Having special needs can happen to anyone at any time.

As a society, we need to better understand the power of this message so we can change the way in which we view and interact with people with disabilities. There is no shame in having a child with special needs, unless you put it there. Don't do that to your child or yourself. You'll regret it later.

It's far too early in the parenting game to give up on your child.

Myth number two: Children with special needs are born only to the poverty-stricken, the mentally ill, those who abuse drugs and alcohol during pregnancy, or moms with poor prenatal care.

The need to blame parents for their children's special needs is common and rarely justified. It does nothing to help families successfully address their demanding new roles. Parents can do everything right during pregnancy and beyond, and life circumstances may still intervene harshly and without permission. During the endless days that my son spent in pediatric intensive care units, I found out how quickly unforeseen circumstances can transform the lives of so-called perfect families into families with special needs. It happens more often than most of us want to believe.

Children with special needs live in families crossing all socioeconomic lines. They are born to the richest and poorest of households, to well-educated parents and high school dropouts. They enter the lives of moms who exercise and eat right and moms who smoke crack during pregnancy. They are born to women over forty and to fourteen-year-old girls.

They join families like mine. As tough as it was to meet all of Eric's needs, I don't feel the least bit cheated, because he taught me so much. When I think of my son today, what I most remember is how much I loved him—and always will

Of the 54 million Americans with special needs, more than 8 million are children and young adults, numbers increasing each year. Many other children have significant needs that may go undiagnosed. Special Olympics (www.specialolympics.org) sites 170 million people worldwide with mental retardation.

You are not alone in this parenting adventure.

Myth number three: Once you have a child with special needs, your life is over.

If you consider your life over because you have a child with special needs, then that's exactly what it will be. Make another choice. Reclaim your personal power and turn a worst-case scenario into something better. Life dreams don't have to end because you have this challenging new parenting role. It does take more energy, more time, and tons of hard work to make your life the best it can be in light of special needs parenting.

But nothing worth having in this life comes easily.

Far too many families end up creating the very prisonlike existence they fear simply because they lack good information, helpful resources, and the positive role models they need to create better outcomes. This book provides you with the necessary tools to create better lives for you and your family. You can use these tools to your advantage to build a life that's still filled with possibilities and personal dreams, or you can become stuck.

Don't become imprisoned in your daily life because your child has special needs, no matter how tough the day may seem. You deserve more—and so does your child.

There has never been a better time to be raising a child with special needs. Many families today are choosing to raise their children as valued family members. These parents have become successful child advocates, nurturing their children's hopes and dreams and fostering independence, just like other families.

You are the beneficiary of all the positive actions of the amazing families who have walked this road before you. With their passionate commitment to their children, they have opened doors once nailed shut and have helped create greater awareness of all children with special needs, including yours. You are fortunate to be following in some amazing parenting footsteps.

You have a responsibility to continue their work—*for the sake of your child*.

I realize that at this moment you may feel like you have been dumped into the middle of a dark, foreboding forest with no apparent way out—especially if your child has just been diagnosed with special needs. Most of us have felt like that at one time or another.

Use this book as your compass, and a breath of fresh air, to help you successfully navigate the special needs parenting woods. With good support, you can find your way.

To become an **increasingly empowered parent** (IEP), read on!

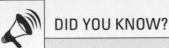 **DID YOU KNOW?**

Special Needs Hall of Fame

Here are just a few famous people with special needs to provide you with some daily parenting inspiration and help you focus on the value of your child:

Dyslexia

Cher	Thomas Edison
Tom Cruise	General George Patton
Walt Disney	

Blindness

Andrea Bocelli	Ray Charles
Stevie Wonder	Helen Keller

Deafness

Heather Whitestone, Former Miss America	Ludwig van Beethoven

Mental Illness*

Lenny Bruce	Sylvia Plath
Judy Garland	Mark Rothko
Ernest Hemingway	Brian Wilson
Charles Mingus	Virginia Woolf
Marilyn Monroe	

Parkinson's Disease

Michael J. Fox	Katharine Hepburn
Muhammad Ali	

Down Syndrome

Christopher Burke

Wheelchair Use

Christopher Reeve	John Hockenberry
Franklin Delano Roosevelt	

*(This list has been drawn from the book *Divine Madness* by Jeffrey Kottler, published by Jossey-Bass/John Wiley & Sons, 2006.)

Information (with the exception of the mental illness list) courtesy of ERIC: Education Resources Information Center/Institute of Education Services of the U.S. Department of Education/ERIC.ed.gov.

SPECIAL TIPS

Here are some tips that you can use right away, immediately after birth or when you receive an unexpected diagnosis of special needs:

- *Believe in your child's value—no matter what.* Every single decision you make to help your child realize his or her full human potential stems from this one powerful belief. Don't ever doubt your child's value!

- *Bond with your child as soon as possible after birth, including in the intensive care unit.* Research strongly indicates that parent-child bonding and human touch may help the most challenged newborns survive and thrive. Don't waste a moment of this critical stage of your child's life. This bonding will pay off as your child grows. Try not to be intimidated by staff—you *are* the child's parent, and you have a right to spend time with that child whenever possible.

- *Send out birth announcements with your child's photograph.* This single, important act helps validate your child's value from birth, while granting others permission to offer congratulations as they would for any other family. Have a photograph taken of your newborn in the hospital, or take it yourself. If your child should die, you will be eternally grateful to have this sacred reminder. Such photos also help you look back to see just how far your child has come developmentally.

- *Encourage visits from supportive family and friends.* The support of those you most trust can prove comforting as you work toward accepting your new parenting role. These supportive visits can also protect you from becoming isolated or depressed, which are concerns for many parents of kids with special needs. This is a great time to reach out to others.

- *Seek out immediate support if you feel overwhelmed.* This support can come from other parents you trust, close friends and family, your faith community, or professional counseling. Learning to ask for help when you need it is an important part of becoming a confident parent of a child with special needs. There is no shame in asking for help. This is a tough adjustment for most families. Don't pretend to be brave.

Special Resources

Here are a few resources to get you started on the path to becoming an **IEP** (increasingly empowered parent!):

Books and Journals

- *The Child with Special Needs: Encouraging Intellectual and Emotional Growth*, by Stanley I. Greenspan, M.D., and Serena Wieder, Ph.D.
- *Asperger's Syndrome: A Guide for Parents and Professionals*, by Tony Attwood.
- *The OASIS Guide to Asperger Syndrome*, by Patricia R. Bashe and Barbara L. Kirby. OASIS online support Web site: www.aspergerssyndrome.org.
- *Behavioral Intervention for Young Children with Autism: A Manual for Parents and Professionals*, by Catherine Murice, Gina Green, and Stephen Luce. Addresses the intensive, expensive, and increasingly popular *applied behavior analysis*.
- *Exceptional Parent Magazine*, www.eparent.com.

Organizations

- Autism Society of America (ASA): www.autism-society.org or 1-800-3-AUTISM. Featuring AutismSource: ASA's national, online directory of autism resources.
- The Doug Flutie Jr. Foundation for Autism, Inc.: www.dougflutiejrfoundation.org.

Internet Search Engine

- www.Google.com. This is a great search engine to help you uncover a wealth of online special needs parenting resources and support throughout your child's life.

Special Note

The Internet is a valuable tool for parent-to-parent networking and accessing important resources. If you don't have a computer, make getting one a priority. If finances are a concern, seek out organizations that now provide computers to those in need. Be proactive.

OK, now you have a better understanding of what it really means to be the parent of a child with special needs—with all its joys and challenges. So let's turn to Chapter Two and continue our discussion about autism. We'll also talk about grief, blame, and asking for help . . .

2

FIRST YOU CRY

In the midst of winter I finally learned there was in me an invincible summer.

—Albert Camus

It can be tough to focus on building better lives for children with special needs when your own life seems ruled by powerful emotions run amok. The wide range of strong and normal feelings that come with a diagnosis of special needs include grief, fear, sadness, anger, disbelief, fatigue, and disappointment. This can make you feel as if you're teetering on the brink of insanity.

Been there. Felt that. Survived!

Welcome to the emotional roller-coaster world of special needs parenting. It's critical to give expression to all of those powerful emotions, which most parents experience at some point throughout their children's lives—especially during an initial diagnosis of special needs and when developmental milestones are delayed or unrealized.

I'm talking about milestones that most families take for granted: sitting up, walking, talking, brushing your teeth, dressing yourself, eating pizza without choking, staying out of the hospital, sleeping through the night, riding a bike, swimming at the beach, taking ballet lessons, playing an instrument, hitting a home run on the Little League team, and starring in the school play. Or being able to write your own name, form meaningful friendships, behave appropriately in a social setting—including in a regular classroom in your neighborhood school, and make the school's honor roll.

Down the road, this list may also include other things: getting a driver's license, going to the prom, playing sports, attending college and having a job, getting married, having children, and living independently or in a group home setting.

Throughout your child's life, you may have to grieve the loss of some big and some small parenting dreams as you incorporate new dreams and expectations. You may be one of those families that has to face the most devastating loss of all—the death of a child—as my family had to. (See Chapter Eight.)

No one said this special needs parenting stuff was easy!

By now, you can probably see why the grief that comes with having a child with special needs is often part of a lifelong, sorting-out process. The good news is that you can learn to recognize and anticipate such grief stages as they approach, allowing you to better address them and then move forward into the uncertain parenting territory that lies ahead.

Don't be fooled into thinking you can ignore grief's impact on your life. The sense of loss that comes with special needs parenting is very real. So be sure to ask for help and reach out to other families of similarly challenged children. There's a healing that comes from connecting with other parents, which is unequaled, and these parents often provide you with valuable networking, helpful resources, and top-notch professional referrals. Tap into this valuable resource early on. *And don't be afraid to cry.*

Releasing *all* of your emotions can help keep you from getting stuck in an ugly and destructive parenting place, where you don't want to be for long, trust me. You do have a choice—and yes, you *can* heal from your sense of loss.

The aim of this chapter is to provide information that can help keep you from living in a permanent state of denial about your child's special needs by giving you *permission* to talk about sensitive issues that most of us would rather not discuss. And then move on. It is tough to move forward when you are stuck in the past. Always move forward!

This may be a good time to throw out all those old, familiar child-development rule books. From now on, you will be asked to write some brand-new parenting guidelines of your own. But do hold on to dear old *Dr. Spock!* It's a timeless and useful parenting resource.

Because the rapidly growing number of children with autism has left many families reeling, we begin this chapter with a second story about parenting a child with autism. Unlike the diagnosis in the Lewis story, the diagnosis in this case is more severe.

In each case, the family is determined to raise their children with dignity.

A SUCCESS STORY

Annie Lewis is used to facing the challenges of raising two sons with the higher-functioning form of autism called Asperger's Syndrome, but Diane and Michael Bubel's child is at the other end of the autism spectrum.

Their fourteen-year-old son, Mike Jr., is profoundly autistic and exhibits many of the classic traits associated with autism. He speaks few words, engages in arm flapping, is sensory challenged, and can be self-injurious.

"Mike is like a darned sponge," Diane Bubel says of the ninth grader. "If the energy level is too high, he will go off the Richter scale and have a meltdown. If we keep everything scheduled and predictable for him, he will be more successful."

First and foremost, Mike is a much-loved son.

"Mike is Mike," Bubel says of her son. "He is his own individual without any regards to societal expectations placed on him by the outside world. He loves the trampoline, and bowling, and swimming for Special Olympics."

Mike loves flash cards and knows his alphabet and numbers front to back, and he loves his videos, especially *Sesame Street*, *Winnie the Pooh*, and *Barney*. "Sameness and consistency in routine are his friends," Bubel says. "That's who Mike is. We accept him 100 percent and we allow him to be who he is."

Today, Diane Bubel is the executive director of the Bubel/ Aiken Foundation (BAF) created by *American Idol* sensation Clay

Aiken to honor the Bubel family and promote societal inclusion of those with developmental disabilities, especially autism.

It began as an independent-study class project required of Aiken to obtain his teaching degree in special education. (For more on Clay Aiken and BAF, see page 242 and visit www.bubelaiken foundation.org.)

Before skyrocketing to superstardom on the second season of the popular television program, Aiken spent a year working with Mike and his family, as a community inclusion specialist, and today they remain in touch.

Aiken had worked with children who were autistic and non-verbal during his days as a substitute teacher.

"Mike was in a terrible middle school situation, acting out and getting aggressive with us. He was hitting and punching and biting," Bubel says.

"Then Clay Aiken walked through the door. He was a perfect fit. He was absolutely the person we needed at that moment in time," she says. "Clay never got frustrated. He cleverly decided that the best way to figure Mike out was to immerse himself in Mike's world. Mike tends to ignore people when he meets them, but little by little, he let Clay in.

"Clay used to sing to Mike in the car all the time, especially after leaving a stressful situation," adds Bubel, who first encouraged Aiken to try out for *American Idol*. "It didn't matter what Mike did. I knew that Clay would be back the next day. He is completely open and comfortable with this population."

Bubel was equally impressed with Aiken's treatment of her daughter, Emma. "He was like a big brother. Not a day went by when Clay didn't sit down and talk with Emma about her life," Bubel says. "He knew it was important to pay attention to her, too.

"Clay Aiken is like a member of our family."

When Mike Bubel was diagnosed with autism at age two, his mom knew something was amiss. Her firstborn, Emma, age fifteen, was an easy child. Mike didn't exhibit typical infant and toddler behavior. He was born two weeks prematurely, refused to breast-feed, and was often ill.

"He was finicky, screamed a lot and had night terrors," Bubel explains. "I was struggling with him." Mike crawled for one day, before going straight to walking. "He was always behind socially and verbally but way ahead physically," Bubel says. "I just chalked it up to being a boy."

When Mike babbled as a toddler but then got silent, Bubel knew he was regressing. She read all the autism books and learned that Mike had every symptom except self-injurious behavior, which came later. "Having an answer set me free," she says. "I was so worried I was the cause.

"I think I grieved before we got the official diagnosis," she says of the news. "My husband and I had a different approach to grieving. It was a bit rocky between us for a while, but I finally said to him, 'You need to get over this because we've got a huge problem here, and we need to work together.'" It was the beginning of new parenting challenges.

"When Mike was first diagnosed, my take was that I was going to try to cure him, fix him, help him be typical," Bubel says. "We did all the popular therapies when he was young," she explains, including two years of *applied behavior analysis*, a form of intervention that provides children with autism with opportunities for maximum learning in structured settings. Success was limited. Mike learned to walk without throwing himself on the ground. "But I realized that he wasn't going to be the one who had the big turnaround.

"When Mike was younger, I was desperately trying to prepare him for this world and trying to change who he was. We had a whole plan in place while he was in preschool, and we did have some small successes." They learned to measure success in other ways. "Getting him toilet trained was a huge accomplishment. I felt that if Mike never did one more thing, I would be a happy woman!

"As Mike has gotten older, I've learned that if I am really going to let him be who he is, I am going to have to compromise." Those compromises included enrolling Mike in a center-based program in North Carolina, where his family lives. It was not their first choice.

Mike attended a regular school from kindergarten through fifth grade, where he was placed in a specialized classroom for kids with autism. "They let him in the building, but he could have been on an island," Bubel says. "He wasn't included in anything." Mike's experiences at the school went from bad to worse.

The difference that the family saw in Mike at the center-based school was immediate and dramatic. "He has actually been more included in the separate school setting than he ever was in the public schools," Bubel says. "The teacher immediately got him involved in clubs, had him walking the hallways with passes, and he even went to the prom. That is totally unheard of in the public schools here for kids like Mike."

With the nationwide push for educational inclusion, Bubel knows that many won't support the family's decision. "When we weighed where we were with the schools in my state, with our understanding of these kids, we decided this was the right decision for Mike right now.

"What we found is a school that works best for him."

She compares it to being involved in Special Olympics. "Mike can't compete in regular community sports programs, but thanks to this wonderful organization, he can now participate in sports, too.

"I am no longer willing to make Mike do things that aren't right for him," Bubel adds. "I'm trying to allow him to be who he is and participate in things he really wants to do instead—and I'm OK with that."

Mike's life has been made more complicated by his lack of speech. "Communication has always been one of our biggest challenges," Bubel says. The family uses picture books to allow Mike to make his own choices. Using technology is a future goal.

Another challenge facing the family is sexuality. That's a tough one Bubel says. They challenge Mike to be aware of what he is doing physically, and sometimes they experience the willfulness of a teenager. "I have to ask myself, is this really his autism or is this how a teenager behaves?"

Bubel is pensive as she contemplates the future. "Our big concern is that the world is not yet ready for Mike. He will be a hard fit, last on your list," she says. "But he has some terrific skills, especially detail work. He can crank out a mailing and enjoy the heck out of it! And he loves repetitive stuff."

She believes Mike will be employable in a sheltered kind of workshop where the energy level isn't too high. "I told my husband that we need to brainstorm now because Mike needs a full life," she says. "If the world isn't ready for him, then we need to get it ready for him.

"I'm not ready to let him go yet," Bubel admits. "Our plan right now is to have him stay with us and possibly set up our own group home." It's a choice more families are making.

Some of the choices Mike's family have made for him are important reminders that as advocates for the rights of those with special needs, we also need to respect a family's right to make decisions that work best for their child—without passing judgment.

"I think I am the greatest spokesperson for the Bubel/Aiken Foundation because I want to make everything available for Mike. I want the schools to be fully inclusive, and I want society to accept our kids for who they are," Bubel says. "If we get there, is Mike going to be able to do it all? No. But he should be able to *choose* whether he does or not. Our challenge is to change the way people view this population," she adds. "We've got to change attitudes before we can change everything else."

UNDERSTANDING AND RESOLVING GRIEF

When most people hear the word grief, they think someone has died. But in the case of special needs, parents are often asked to deal with a different kind of grief, one that often has no clear ending because it recurs as parenting dreams and predictable developmental milestones are lost or delayed.

Although your grief may also involve the physical death of a child, as it has in my family, it is likely you will find yourself grieving the losses of a child who is still very much alive.

This reality feels unnatural and makes parents uncomfortable. It just doesn't feel right grieving someone who's living. Yet there will be times when that is exactly what you must do in order to let

DIANE BUBEL'S TIPS

Parents

Diane Bubel shares three key strategies for parenting a child with autism:

- *Hang in there.* "Early on, you aren't sure you can handle this responsibility, but I wouldn't change a thing about this experience. We are a better family. I am a better mother. My husband is a better dad. Emma is a better sister. We are all better people because of Mike. This isn't a pie-in-the-sky experience, but the journey has been well worth it. We are what we are, and Mike has taught me that's OK."

- *Have a sense of humor.* "It's OK to laugh at a crisis situation. This is the life you have. You either live with it or you are miserable with it. I chose to live with it and be joyful."

- *Slow down and fall in love with your child.* "Figure out how to be your child's mother or father. You don't always have to be his teacher or therapist. You can just be his soft place to land. Enjoy your child—let him be who he is. We have learned to love Mike for who he is."

go of your former parenting expectations and embrace new parenting dreams. It's part of the necessary sorting-out process that helps you come to terms with the child you have. It can be a delicate emotional balancing act for many families.

Many grief experts, most notably Elisabeth Kübler-Ross in *On Grief and Grieving*, describe the five familiar stages of grief that typically follow a death: denial and isolation, anger, bargaining, depression, and acceptance. Many of these stages are also present in the grief of families of children with special needs, so some traditional grief resources will be helpful for you as you work to understand and resolve your own sense of loss. A few of these books are listed in the resource section at the end of this chapter on pages 55–56.

But because I believe strongly in using language that is easily understood by all, and I find healing power in adding humor whenever possible, I've come up with my own ten key tips for special needs parenting grief.

I hope my simple, heartfelt words help you understand your own grief just a bit better.

 ## JUDY WINTER'S TIPS

Stages of Parenting Grief

Taken from my own experiences and the experiences of other parents brave enough to share with me, here are my ten key stages of parenting grief:

- *The what-the-heck-just-happened-to-us? stage.* This is the diagnosis stage, with lots of heavy denial and possibly overwhelming desperation. Shell-shocked behavior (think deer in the headlights) is also common during this stage. This is when you receive your first serious jolt of parenting reality, with the surprising news that *your child is not perfect.* Now what are you supposed to do with such news? (Reading this book is a good place to start.)

- *The this-really-stinks stage.* This is the anger and denial stage, with lots of guilt, blame, fear, depression, lack of sleep, and plenty of accusations to go around. It may also turn into the following related stage.

  The I-want-to-run-away-from-home-for-good-because-I'm-only-human stage. My advice is to go ahead and run away from home for brief periods of time, but make sure that your child is well taken care of and that you come back within a reasonable amount of time. At this stage, even

(continued on next page)

(*continued from previous page*)

short escapes can work wonders. I remember taking lots of long drives in the country and yelling some not very nice things at God, for which I later apologized. This is a good time to seek professional help if you are struggling.

- *The I-know-I-can-do-this stage.* This is the beginning of real acceptance. The dust has begun settling around you, and you can see your parenting reality a bit more clearly. By this time, you'll have also put some things into place to help you move forward more positively into the next parenting stage, like early-on prevention services, the support of family and friends and other parents, and access to good doctors and other top-notch professionals. You don't stumble as much while walking down familiar streets.

- *The I'm-back-in-charge-of-my-life-now stage.* Warning! This stage is often temporary. The danger here comes from falsely believing you can now go back to life exactly as it was before your child was born. But unless your child's special needs are very minor, your life and everything about it has changed, and the old life rules probably won't work.

- *The I-have-to-make-tough-choices stage.* I can still recall the day that I had to choose between keeping the job I loved with PBS and taking care of my child. I faced a no-choice choice. My life had changed drastically. My decisions needed to reflect that change if I was to have a brighter future. I gave up the job that I loved to help my child have a better life. That decision still stings today— but my son's life, and mine, turned out much better as a result.

- *The I'm-becoming-increasingly-less-selfish stage.* It's common for one parent to give up employment to stay home and take care of the special needs child, particularly when the child is young. You become less self-centered for the sake of your child's future, which is no easy feat in our narcissistic society. But it can lead to parenting success. Helping children with special needs reach their full potential is a full-time job. If you must work, consider working part time, taking on the night shift, or freelancing (as I've done). Where there's a will, there is usually a compromise—especially as your child gets older.

- *The preparing-for-what's-next stage*. During this stage, you begin addressing your child's present and future needs in earnest. This is the beginning of taking on true advocacy. Ideally, it's also the beginning of less sleep deprivation. Warning! The return of some of those annoying type A personality traits is possible during this increasingly confident stage. Try not to embrace their return. They will only exhaust, disappoint, and derail you. Believe me, I know.

- *The I-love-my-child-no-matter-what-happens-next stage*. One day, you begin to realize that rather than feel cheated as a parent, you are in love with your child after all and would do anything for him or her. This is the beginning of lifelong advocacy and unconditional love for your child—also known as the *Mommy* or *Papa Lion Stage*. You would kill for your child.

- *The my-idea-of-family-has-changed-and-that's-OK stage*. Your sense of humor begins to reemerge, along with a possible social life and a diet consisting of something besides fast-food burgers and fries. You may even have time to whip up a few home-cooked meals. Maybe. This doesn't mean it's all so much easier to handle; it just means you have begun experiencing the true joys of

(continued on next page)

(continued from previous page)

parental bonding, and you see your child as more than just a burden. This child has become a part of your family, one that has been redefined, but one no less valuable than any other.

- *The I've-accepted-things-as-they-are stage.* This is the *magical moment of acceptance*, especially when you realize that if given the opportunity, you would not give up your child for any reason, no matter how tough the day. At this stage, the love between parent and child begins to grow in earnest, allowing you to meet new parenting challenges head on. Reaching this stage says a lot about how far you have come as a special needs parent. It helps set the solid foundation for all future advocacy. This acceptance stage may come earlier for some families than for others, but with hard work, a solid commitment to connecting with your child, and lots of hugs and kisses, it will come. When it does, it's magical! Savor it.

Addressing Grief Issues

I hope you now see that even though parenting a child with special needs is serious stuff, it's also important not to take it so darn seriously all the time. Otherwise it can prove overwhelming.

Laughter is a healthy stress release and one I strongly recommend.

In fact, the previous tips were designed to help you address your new parenting role with the least amount of grief possible. It's OK to still laugh. It helps keep you sane! Many times, you'll be laughing at the absurdity of your demands.

As you begin this challenging parenting journey, I want you to know that had I been given the choice to erase my son's disability, I would have done so in a heartbeat, so that *Eric* would not have had to go through all the tough, often inexcusable stuff he experienced daily. I would never have changed him just to make my life easier (big difference!). Because then, Eric would not have been the child I came to know and love deeply, and I would not be the person I am today, someone of whom I am proud. Eric taught me many things, but here's one of his greatest lessons: in all his imperfection, my son was *perfect* just the way he was.

I hope this is your experience, too.

 DID YOU KNOW?

Kids make great special needs advocates, too!

On June 12, 2005, Chris Pentescu, an eleven-year-old with Type 1 (juvenile) diabetes, led a team of cyclists in Brighton, Michigan, to help raise money for the annual *Tour de Cure* race for the American Diabetes Association. In Fall 2002, the spirited fifth grader also served as a youth ambassador for the annual America's Walk for Diabetes.

"I want to do whatever I can to help find a cure—and to help spread the word about diabetes. It doesn't matter if I'm a kid. Kids can have a lot to say," Chris says of his advocacy. "I want adults to listen and learn about diabetes."

According to the American Diabetes Association Web site, 18.2 million Americans have some form of diabetes. To find out more about this serious disease that often goes undetected, visit www.diabetes.org or www.jda.org. Check it out. Way to go, Chris!!

Avoiding Guilt and Blame

Playing the blame game is pretty familiar to most parents of children with special needs (although they may deny it). Many of us want to know exactly what went wrong and why and how we could have prevented it. As if we were really that powerful. We aren't, but we can choose how we *react* to our situations. That's true parenting power.

The realization that special needs can rudely invade our lives, often without warning, is a concept so disturbing and painful to most families that they need to hold someone or something accountable.

We need a target toward which to vent our rage and lack of acceptance, a target that often includes God. Unfortunately, casting blame, harboring guilt, and targeting faith rarely solve parenting dilemmas and often succeed only in making us more miserable and less able to cope. It is exhausting to be angry all the time. I don't recommend it for anyone.

In many cases, there may be no clear answer as to why your child has special needs. In the rare case that there is one, little or nothing will be solved from harboring strong feelings that can do nothing to change the reality of your situation except keep you stuck and angry.

You are being asked to face the reality of having a child with special needs—for whatever reason. And you may also be asked to forgive *big time*.

What are you going to do about it? It's far better to use your precious energy to make good parenting decisions that affect your child's future and your own in more productive ways than to stay in denial. It's not an easy choice to make, especially when people around you are looking for a cause for this perceived tragedy to help themselves feel less vulnerable.

But it sure beats the alternative!

Releasing Powerful Emotions Safely

That said, if you must vent your rage in all its ugliness, try to do it in a way that is not destructive to you and others. And please don't do it in front of your children—or *to* your children! There is no excuse good enough to ever defend hurting a child, no matter how overwhelmed or sleep deprived you may be. If you are in danger of turning your anger on your child, walk away, take a break, or seek professional help NOW!

Here are a few suggestions to help you vent powerful emotions safely, before they become overwhelming:

- *Write down every single ugly word you feel about your new role in a journal.* Use whatever language is necessary, then burn the pages and try not to revisit them. Journal your thoughts whenever you feel the need. It is a healing, inexpensive, and safe way to get your feelings out.

- *Write a letter to whomever or whatever you think has done you wrong.* But don't mail it. Rip it up instead. Getting words on paper is a good release and often makes you feel better, which may make it easier to forgive. It's tiring carrying all those strong emotions around. You can't make room for new stuff when you are holding on tightly to all the old garbage.

- *Break old plates or scream into pillows, go work out at the gym, take up boxing or martial arts or weight lifting, or go for a run or a long, brisk walk daily.* These are all great stress relievers and you might even lose some weight!

- *Don't be afraid to get angry with God.* I'm pretty sure he can handle it. Faith can be an important coping tool in life, especially when you are working hard to forgive others. Try to move beyond anger, embrace your faith, and forgive, whatever your beliefs.

Harboring unresolved anger, guilt, and blame will solve nothing and may cost you everything. Instead start rebuilding your life from the ashes (if you must view your child's special needs that way), but build it up, don't tear it down. You are going to need all your precious parenting energy to make good decisions for your child now and in the future.

Don't waste it.

ASK FOR THE SUPPORT YOU NEED

Throughout this book, you will hear one message repeated over and over again in the hope that one important message sticks in your brain: *it's OK to ask for help*.

Most of us pride ourselves on being so darn self-sufficient. We like to think we're so tough that we can pick ourselves up by our bootstraps from the worst life blows, shake off the dust, and go back into the ring for another round of knockout punches—before going out for pizza.

We make some crazy choices, don't we? We live in a world in which we are encouraged to go back to work on the Monday following the Friday funeral of a loved one, straight from a wake at which most of us behave as if we are at a cocktail party. We are really good at saying we're OK when asked by others who are concerned, when we are clearly not. There is no room in special needs parenting for pretending that you are tough as nails and can handle everything that comes your way all alone. You can't.

Let me repeat this: *you can't handle this all by yourself*—at least not for very long. You will burn out, become bitter, or pay a physical price for this decision. You are human!

In most cases, any one of the physical, spiritual, and emotional demands of special needs parenting is enough to deplete your energy and make you scream uncle. You need to remember that your new responsibility *is* for life. Wise parents take advantage of whatever support comes their way and ration their energy and parenting reserves.

Think of it as running a marathon: pace yourself, so you can finish. Don't be afraid to accept offers of support, like a home-cooked meal, a night out (baby-sitting included), or a friend's listening ear or supportive shoulder. These are the very things that can help you make it through the next twenty-four hours, the next major illness, the next hospitalization, the next bad medical news, or the next sleepless night.

Accept these gifts as they come, and don't be afraid to ask for them. They can help you gain the much-needed perspective that may prove elusive. When friends and relatives ask you how they can be of support, don't be shy. Tell them! Ask if they would do your laundry, pick up milk and bread, meet your child after school, or provide a hot meal on Tuesday night. It's OK to accept the help of others. You can return the favor to someone in need down the road. Everybody gets an opportunity to be supported and to support others in life. Most people want to help in some way; they just don't know how. Help teach them by allowing them to share in answering the challenges of your family. The more you ask for help, the better you get at it! Just don't abuse the honor.

Facing Lengthy and Repeated Hospitalizations

When it comes to repeated hospitalizations, I'm the voice of far too much experience. During the first two years of my son's life, Eric faced nearly twenty-five hospitalizations, most of them in the pediatric intensive care unit.

The longest stay was nearly a month, so staying out of the hospital became our mission. If we were home for more than two weeks, we thought we'd won the lottery. During those early years, we spent almost as much time at the hospital as we did in our house.

More than once, Eric's medical condition was critical enough to warrant our concern that he might not survive, so we didn't want to leave his side. It was one of the most stressful periods of our lives. Still, we were determined to see Eric through it with the least amount of physical and emotional trauma possible.

I loved my son with every ounce of my being, from day one, but there were times early on when I felt like I was in prison, with no chance of parole. During that uncertain phase of Eric's life, I found myself advocating for proper pain medication in the recovery room when a far-too-green medical student was far too tentative after a tough surgery. I watched my son have an IV put into his head when the veins in his arms and legs had all collapsed, while I was still wearing heavy makeup from my shift begging for money during one of those long PBS pledge drives. Talk about a reality check—and a humbling one at that. During this intense life phase, it pays to hang in there—and hang on tightly.

Here are a few of my time-tested tips to help you make the hospitalization phase a bit more tolerable. They worked for my family—maybe they'll work for yours.

JUDY WINTER'S TIPS

Surviving Hospital Stays

The following parent-tested tips (mine!) might help you keep your sanity intact when your child is hospitalized:

- *Introduce yourself to the hospital staff.* You may be seeing lots of each other.

- *Ask the staff not to speak loudly at your child's bedside while the child is sleeping.* Ask them to help you prevent unwanted visitors during those times by placing a *Shh-hhh. Child Sleeping!* note on the door and at the nurse's station.

- *Ask for a rocking chair so you can comfortably rock your child, especially babies and young children.* Don't be surprised if they are hard to come by. If I had my way, there would be one in every room of a child under the age of five. Be persistent.

- *Nap while your child is sleeping.* In fact, sleep whenever you can.

- *Wash your hands often and well to avoid passing on germs.* These germs could possibly keep your child (and you) in the hospital longer than necessary.

- *Ask family and friends to visit you in the hospital, unless* they *are sick.* Remember, even a little cold may compromise the health of a child with special needs.

- *Whenever possible, ask that your child be reassigned to nurses who have already worked with your family.* This will help provide consistency in care and reduce unnecessary stress. It never hurts to ask.

- *Take turns covering day and overnight hospital shifts with your partner or others.* This will help you avoid burnout and will enable you to spend uninterrupted time with your other children.

- *Go home to sleep whenever your child is in the intensive care unit and receiving close attention.* Sleep is priceless! You will feel less comfortable doing this when your child is on a regular floor with less one-on-one coverage (make sure you can be reached).

- *Avoid overindulging in caffeine, alcohol, too many sweets, or too much cafeteria food.* Of course, there will be days when eating the fried chicken, mashed potatoes, and chocolate pie will be the highlight of your day! Make healthier food choices to help keep your energy level and mood up. Walk around the hallways or outdoors to keep from going stir crazy and to relieve stress and keep up an exercise routine (however modified). Even a few minutes helps.

- *Keep a journal.* This is something you can do when you are spending time in the family lounge, during lengthy procedures or surgeries, or during long hours spent at a sleeping child's bedside.

- *Remember to take care of sibling needs.* If you decide to take your other children to the hospital (when appropriate or allowed), bring along crayons, books, snacks, or homework, especially on weekends when you want to include some family time in those long stays.

(continued on next page)

(continued from previous page)

- *If you know a hospitalization is coming, prepare food ahead of time.* This way, you'll have ready-made healthy meals on hand to help sustain you. This is also a great time to accept offers of home-cooked meals from family or friends. Don't be afraid to beg—and never turn down food. Freeze it.

- *Request regular visits from your pastor or priest or request to see a hospital chaplain.* Most hospital chaplains serve all patients, regardless of beliefs or denomination or church attendance. They can provide a welcome and nonjudgmental listening ear (at no additional charge) and help address crisis-intervention needs, as can social workers, who are often involved in aftercare home planning. Access these services as needed.

Now that you have some tools to help you through this challenging phase, here's one final word of advice. During my son's many hospitalizations, we received some great medical care from some incredible professionals with great hearts—especially those amazing and often-overworked nurses. Thank God for all the Florence Nightingales of the world!

I could not have made it through this stage without all the outstanding professionals who helped us have our son with us for a much longer period of time than we might have otherwise. For that, I will be forever grateful.

Treat these individuals well. There's a good chance you'll be seeing them again.

Depending on your child's needs—as with most phases of special needs parenting—it helps to recite this one powerful parenting mantra: *this stage too shall pass.*

The good news is that for most families, it probably will.

SPECIAL TIPS

Here are some suggestions on how you can face the many challenges that may greet you on this often rocky parenting journey:

- *Give yourself permission to grieve.* Seek out whatever support you need to address and resolve your feelings about having a child with special needs.

- *Let the tears flow.* Crying is nature's way of helping us heal in a healthy way from a devastating loss or emotional blow—and this is a big one. Tears can be especially important during those early days when you may feel overwhelmed with your child's diagnosis, especially if it comes at birth when your own hormones may still be raging. You won't cry forever and tears are a great stress release. The support you need can come from many sources, including grief books, writing in journals, a fitness plan, family, friends, your faith community, or professional counseling. Not only is it OK to ask for help, it's healthy! When it comes to special needs parenting, it pays to learn this lifesaving rule early on.

- *Try to ignore people who tell you what you should not be feeling.* If you are feeling it, then you need to own it and deal with it. Unless others have walked in your shoes, they can't possibly know what you are going through.

- *Stop asking Why?* There are rarely answers to this nagging, persistent question, and continuing to ask it will keep you stuck in the past. Even if there is an answer, *it won't change the reality of your child's special needs.* Better to use the valuable energy wasted on this question to work toward creating a better future for your child and your family.

- *Draw strength from your faith, instead of blaming God for what has happened.* This shift in spiritual thinking may help you more successfully address your challenges and more easily accept your child. Prayer can be a powerful, healing tool, whatever your faith. I would be lost without it.

- *Network with other parents, especially those with a child with similar challenges, or consider joining a support group.* Choose such support carefully. Far too many groups have a tendency to become nothing more than angry, self-pity sessions that will bring you down, not build you up. You want to take part in the kind of affirmative interactions that will help you stay positive, not in those that keep you stuck in bad places. Shop around and if you don't like what you see or hear, keep looking or form your own support group, with clear rules and expectations.

- *Introduce yourself to other families whose children are in the hospital at the same time as your child.* Many families of children with special needs are in the hospital a lot and may prove a great source for networking and useful information, not to mention the socialization aspect that helps make repeated stays less isolating and more tolerable.

- *Keep good medical records.* Begin keeping track of important medical information. Doing this on a computer makes it easy to update and helps make life easier when you must bring professionals up to speed on your child's medical history. Handing over a copy of a well-recorded medical history of your child, including allergies, dates of childhood inoculations, surgeries, and other medical treatment will save you from having to repeat this information every time your child is hospitalized or sees a new physician or other professional. This is a great way to conserve valuable energy, especially during a medical crisis, when you may feel anxious, distraught, or exhausted and don't want to deal with repetitive and sometimes seemingly inane questions often asked in hospitals.

- *Focus on what you can change, not on what you can't change.* Make decisions that will help your child have a better life no matter what challenges face you and no matter how small the decision may seem at the time. There's a good chance it will pay off later.

Special Resources

Here are a few resources to help you become an increasingly empowered parent.

Organizations

- Diane Bubel/The Bubel/Aiken Foundation (BAF): www.thebubelaikenfoundation.com.
- Muscular Dystrophy Association (MDA): www.mdausa.org.
- Elizabeth Glaser Pediatric AIDS Foundation: www.pedaids.org.
- Joni and Friends: the disability ministry of Joni Eareckson Tada: www.joniandfriends.org.

Books

- *The Autism Book: Answers to Your Most Pressing Questions*, by Dawn Ham-Kucharski and S. Jhoanna Robledo.
- *Special Kind of Love: For Those Who Love Children with Special Needs*, by Susan Titus Osborn and Janet Lynn Mitchell.
- *You Will Dream New Dreams: Inspiring Personal Stories by Parents of Children with Disabilities*, by Stanley D. Klein, M.D.
- *Dr. Spock's Baby and Child Care* (8th ed.), and *The First Two Years: The Emotional and Physical Needs of Children from Birth to Age Two*, by Benjamin Spock, M.D.

For Grief and Inspiration

- *Life Is Hello, Life Is Goodbye: Grieving Well Through All Kinds of Loss*, by Alla Bozarth-Campbell.
- *Healing After Loss: Daily Meditations for Working Through Grief*, by Martha Whitmore Hickman.

- *A Time to Grieve: Meditations for Healing After the Death of a Loved One*, by Carol Staudacher.

- *Transitions: Prayers and Declarations for a Changing Life*, and *Answered Prayers: Love Letters from the Divine*, by Julia Cameron.

Special Note

To help you ward off self-pity and replace it with the positive energy and inspiration of others, network with other families of children with special needs. I guarantee that it won't take long before you find parents who seem to have it worse than you do but are handling their challenges well. Pick their brains and discover their survival secrets. Hearing another family's story doesn't diminish the reality of your own situation, but it may help you feel better about it, which *can* help you survive the toughest days. A positive attitude *does* make a difference when facing the demands of special needs parenting, and the understanding and support of other parents often provide a much-welcomed emotional boost.

OK, now you've got permission to address grief issues and other powerful emotional challenges, so let's move on to Chapter Three—and discover the value of embracing hope, avoiding limiting labels, and dealing with staring. To learn more about the power of thinking outside the parenting box, just turn the page.

3

NO LABELS, YES HOPE

Once we have labeled the things around us, we do not bother
to look at them so carefully.

—Jane Goodall

Of all the challenges facing parents of children with special
needs, few are as frustrating as the negative labels and reduced
expectations placed on our children by a society that often devalues them. Labels like retard, idiot, spastic, Mongoloid, stupid, slow,
mental, problem child, and many others do little to lift our children
up in the minds of society—or even in our own.

Most families hate labels, and rightly so. After all, that's somebody's son, daughter, brother, sister, grandson, granddaughter,
cousin, nephew, niece, and friend that people are talking about in
some not-so-flattering ways. That's your flesh and blood. How dare
people be so cruel, rude, and insensitive!

Unfortunately, too many people still believe all those outdated
stereotypes about the limitations that come with special needs—in
short, what your child *can't* do, before they even get to know the
child. Most of these infuriating folks don't know any better.

Here's my advice for dealing with them: whenever possible, give
people the benefit of the doubt and chalk up their ignorant and
arrogant misdeeds to a lack of experience, education, or professional
training. There may be times when you prefer to deck someone—
I've felt that way myself.

A far better approach is to take a really deep breath and see
yourself as a wise sage chosen to teach all those who cross your path

on the way to enlightenment about kids with special needs and about parenting them.

This chapter will challenge you to change your *own* focus first: from disability to *ability*. You will learn the importance of embracing hope, how to deal with staring, and why it's important to avoid using limiting labels and negative language.

You will again be reminded of the powerful role that family plays in a child's success and how your actions can help change the negative perceptions of others. Never forget this. It's powerful stuff.

Your special needs parenting work is now beginning in earnest.

So let's get inspired with the remarkable story about a talented artist with Down syndrome—a tale that will have you telling everybody you meet what children with special needs *can* do.

A SUCCESS STORY

Carrie Clise is a successful greeting-card artist, whose work has appeared in *People* magazine. She also has Down syndrome (DS) and the mental capabilities of a five-year-old child. So much for *disability!*

The charming, twenty-one-year-old loves to draw angels, like the *Garden Angel* and the *Angel with a Magic Wand*. Carrie has drawn birds and birdhouses, young girls fishing in boats, best friends holding balloons in wheelchairs, and a bride and groom, complete with wedding gown and tux. There's even a drawing of Baby Jesus wearing a diaper. Her artwork is simple, whimsical, and enchanting. So is Carrie's story about the power of focusing on a child's individual *ability*. "Carrie has a different perspective on the world," says her mom and biggest champion, Rae Clise. "After we grow up, we lose that childlike innocence, but Carrie still perceives the world as a wonderful place."

Carrie's childlike innocence is reflected in simple black-and-white drawings that take her just fifteen minutes to create, using a black ink pen from Wal-Mart—giving a whole new meaning to the term *artist's etchings!*

According to Suzanne Armstrong, director of communications for the National Down Syndrome Society, Carrie is one of 5,000 children born with Down syndrome in the United States each year. "More than 350,000 people in the U.S. have Down syndrome," Armstrong says. "But millions more are impacted by the diagnosis."

Down syndrome is a genetic condition caused by a chromosomal abnormality—an extra twenty-first chromosome—which results in developmental delays due to cognitive disability. According to the National Down Syndrome Society (NDSS), the IQ of most people with this condition is in the mild to moderate range of mental retardation.

Carrie Clise has been diagnosed with Trisomy 21, the most common form of DS. The condition affects people of all races and economic status, Armstrong says, and the additional genetic material that causes DS can originate with either the father or mother.

Women who are age thirty-five-plus have a greater risk of giving birth to children with Down syndrome. The risk increases to one in thirty-five for moms age forty-five and older. Armstrong cites promising new research regarding the medical concerns that come with this diagnosis, including an increased risk of leukemia, Alzheimer's, and heart disease. Fifty percent of babies born with DS have some form of congenital heart defect. "Scientists have now decoded the twenty-first chromosome and are looking at the role each individual gene plays," Armstrong explains.

With the exception of a hearing loss in one ear, Carrie has avoided many of the health concerns associated with Down syndrome. With improved medical treatments and greater awareness, 80 percent of children with DS may now live to age fifty-five or longer, making long-term family planning critical. According to the NDSS, the average life expectancy for someone with DS is now 56.

"The first thing we say to families who contact us for support is 'Congratulations!' because their baby is a baby first and foremost," Armstrong stresses. "Then we tell them we are here to provide them with the information, resources, and support they need throughout their children's lives."

At age twenty-seven, Rae Clise wasn't at risk for having a child with Down syndrome when she gave birth to Carrie more than twenty years ago. Little was known about DS then, but Carrie's parents made a life-altering decision to take her home and raise her as a valued member of their family when they could have chosen to have her institutionalized. "I firmly believe that if Carrie isn't welcome somewhere, then neither am I," Clise says.

She hasn't always felt this way. "My initial reaction when my child was born was that if something was wrong with Carrie, I didn't want her," Clise admits. "Children with special needs are a gift. But it can be hard to see that early on."

Clise credits a skilled, caring pediatrician for answering all her questions about this unexpected diagnosis. "He told us to take Carrie home and raise her as we would any other child."

As Clise talks about her daughter today, her eyes fill with tears in an emotional expression of one mother's unconditional love for her daughter. "At one point, I would have sold my soul to the devil to have a normal child," she says honestly. "But not now, because I love Carrie just the way she is."

That's a powerful statement of *acceptance* for all families to consider. Clise proudly recalls the first time she recognized her daughter's budding artistic talent, at age six. "Carrie painted a watercolor on the cardboard that comes with little boys' underwear," her mom says, laughing. "So I had it matted and framed and hung it in my living room."

Others may have easily dismissed Carrie's artwork as nothing more than an example of false hope, a grieving parent's wish to see talent that didn't exist. But Carrie's teacher also recognized and nurtured Carrie's exceptional talent. Michigan special educator Sue Rundborg oversees a successful school-to-work program (more about that in Chapter Four) for young adults with special needs. "My job is to get my students ready for the real world," she says.

Like Carrie's family, Rundborg chose to look beyond the label of Down syndrome to focus on language that better recognized her student's talent—that of an *artist*. The results were impressive.

Rundborg convinced Carrie's family to turn their child's charming etchings into a (now successful) greeting-card business called Carrie's Cards. "You can't tell Carrie what to draw because she already has it in her mind," says Rundborg, who packaged Carrie's cards in plastic Baggies and test-marketed them at the school's annual holiday bazaar. "They were a huge hit!" she says.

More than twenty years after she was born into a world that often underestimates the potential of children with special needs, Carrie Clise has a thriving greeting-card company—complete with business cards and the word *owner* after her name. That's what I call celebrating *ability!*

Embracing Hope

Carrie's story is a great example of embracing hope, not denying it. It also drives home the importance of refusing to accept limiting labels that can overshadow a child's individual gifts and potential.

Unfortunately, not enough families are told *what's possible* for children with special needs, making it tough for them to embrace hope in their own lives. I wrote this book because I was outraged to find so many children and families living lives of desperation because they believed all the negative hype being spouted about their children.

Many families have lost hope. My mission is to help restore that hope. It's no wonder their dreams prove elusive, when so many families are fed condescending and arrogant words from a variety of professionals working with their children, including physicians, specialists, and educators: words like, "I don't want to give you false hope" and "you need to deal with reality." To this day, I'm still not sure exactly what either of those statements really means. Whose definition of *reality* and whose *hope* are we talking about here anyway?

The false hope excuse is a familiar one often cited by professionals when they find themselves struggling to find something good to say about your child. I'm pretty sure that liability enters in here, too. By using limiting words, citing the scariest statistics, and re-fusing to share family success stories (or even ask for their permission to share them!), professionals risk taking away *all* hope—and your reason to get out of bed in the morning. Don't buy into this hopeless-case scenario. Listen to the *facts*, then explore what's possible for *your* child.

Your child is not a medical statistic, but a unique and valuable human being! I'll take the tiniest ray of hope if it helps me improve a child's life over a doomsday scenario that stops me dead in my parenting tracks any day. Tell me my child has beautiful eyes—something! It's a whole lot easier to get out of bed and face the daily demands of a child with special needs when you can focus on the child's strengths and how to build on them. Christopher Reeve said, "Once we choose hope, everything is possible."

It may help you understand that one big reason that statistics for children with special needs have been so dire is because our past expectations were so low. Years ago, these kids didn't have access to dynamic early intervention services or a disability rights movement and laws fueling educational and societal inclusion—and many of these children were institutionalized. Nobody was giving these kids much of a chance to prove what they *could* do—*if* they thought about them at all.

Let's write a new parenting chapter focusing on *ability*, shall we?

I'm challenging you to create more hopeful future statistics by **raising the bar of expectations** for your child, starting right now! Let's just see where your child ends up with lots of hard work, good programs, and unconditional love. The future of many of these children may still be up for grabs.

The one reality you *must* face is your child's medical diagnosis. If you pretend that your child doesn't have special needs when he does, you will lose valuable parenting time. Gently (but firmly) pull your head out of the parenting sand and seek out a firm diagnosis as soon as you suspect something isn't quite right with your child's development. Be persistent—and trust your parenting gut. It's rarely wrong.

I had to come to terms with the fact that despite giving my child access to the best, most innovative programs available to address his physical challenges, Eric wasn't going to walk independently, and he would require the assistance of a wheelchair to move around. That didn't dash my hope for him.

Many people, including educators (a reality that still shocks me), erroneously labeled our son as mentally impaired based on his degree of physical involvement before they even got to know him.

Why? Because statistically, children with severe physical involvement tend to be cognitively challenged, too. Our son was a bright exception to a pretty dismal statistical rule. We fought a powerful bias against him by not buying into it—and instead nurturing his entire being.

We gave Eric every opportunity to prove the critics wrong and to exhibit his intelligence and abilities through participation in dynamic intervention programs, access to general education, and the pursuit of objective professional assessments—the results of which showed Eric's cognitive abilities as being *at least* age appropriate.

Throughout Eric's life, we did whatever was necessary to successfully address his needs, while working to reduce or eliminate the use of restrictive labeling. Because we focused on his true value, not just words, Eric accomplished a great deal. It took tremendous energy, focus, and firm resolve to fight against potentially damaging labels and limiting language. It was worth every ounce of effort. Being hopeful is a choice. Whenever possible, embrace it!

Here's a brief example of how others may try to dash your hope, especially early on. I'm warning you now so you can be prepared.

- You may be discouraged from having your child attend her neighborhood school in favor of enrolling in a more segregated, center-based program.

- You may be told to forget about all those lofty dreams you've held about your child attending Harvard, scaling Mount Everest, becoming a lawyer, writer, entrepreneur, artist, politician, dancer, famous musician, baseball pitcher, scientist, television journalist, athlete, stand-up comedian, opera singer, cartoonist, award-winning Hollywood actor, or president of the United States.

Good news! People with special needs have accomplished all of these things and will continue to raise societal expectations of them in the future: with your help! For millions of children with special needs, the possibility of leading increasingly independent lives has never looked brighter.

Got hope? Embrace it, don't deny it!

AVOIDING USE OF LIMITING LABELS AND LANGUAGE

Most of us are familiar with that annoying childhood rhyme: "Sticks and stone can break my bones . . . But words can never hurt me." But words do hurt. They can make us feel good or bad, worthwhile or worthless, self-confident or send us running for cover. They can make us laugh or cry, celebrate or grieve, stand up and cheer or fall to our knees. Words are especially powerful when used to describe the abilities of children. Unfortunately, the words often chosen to describe kids with special needs are rarely those that enhance self-esteem or celebrate their abilities.

Here's an example of just some of the words people use to describe children with special needs. Heck, we use them carelessly just for sport to put down people *without* special needs. Shame on us!

Retard (a favorite of teens, also modeled by young Hollywood with absolutely no clue as to why it's so offensive), Mongoloid, idiot, spastic, problem child, sickly child, out-of-control and wild child, crippled, lame, crazy, and one of my all time favorites: the *spec-ed kids*—the shorter, not-so-flattering version describing children who receive special education services.

Do any of these words make you think class valedictorian, CEO of a Fortune 500 company, or Rhodes Scholar? I didn't think so.

Even the most flattering labels, like pretty child, outgoing child, responsible child, good girl, charmer, jock, class clown, over-achiever, leader, the brain, gifted, scholar, smart child, funny child, athletic child, popular child, or shining star, can create unfair pressure for children to become what others perceive them to be, good or bad. Did you realize that language is so powerful? Please, keep that in mind and make better word choices.

With the exception of an official medical diagnosis (such as cerebral palsy, autism, obsessive-compulsive disorder, or muscular dystrophy) required for accessing early intervention programs and services, try to avoid all labels.

And if you must use labels in some circumstances, seek out the least-restrictive labels possible for your child. My son's official medical diagnosis was cerebral palsy, with the additional label of *physically or otherwise health impaired*, for the purpose of all that yearly special education paperwork—a tolerable label that we requested.

Fortunately, the professional use of many outdated and negative labels is now being reassessed. But much work remains before we can celebrate language that builds up all children. Be prepared to advocate for additional changes whenever necessary throughout your child's life.

Labels belong on soup cans, not children.

JUDY WINTER'S TIPS
Language Use

Here are some tips to help you replace all that hurtful, destructive language with words that help build people up.

- *Use the most current, up-to-date terminology for those with special needs* (hint: it's not handicapped, retard, or crippled). *Special needs*, *exceptionalities*, and *disabilities* are the words most often used today to describe our children. Reserve the term *handicapped* for nonhuman stuff like handicapped parking.

(continued on next page)

(continued from previous page)

- Seek out the least restrictive labeling possible for your child. Be aware of what a label means before agreeing to it. Some of these words may have a lifelong negative impact on your child.

- *Use proper terminology when addressing a child's diagnosis, and place all descriptive terms after the child's name.* Which one creates a more positive image in your mind: *Carrie Clise, the artist who has Down syndrome,* or *that Down's kid, Carrie Clise?* Some difference, right?

- *Don't even mention disability when speaking about a child if it isn't necessary.* Disability is only one part of who someone is. Don't make it the most defining one. It may limit a child's life choices. Don't say that a child is *confined* to a wheelchair. The child is a wheelchair *user.* How do children take a shower, use a restroom, or sleep? Children are not *attached* to wheelchairs. Don't make it sound as if they are! And don't say Johnny *suffers* from cerebral palsy. How do you know he's suffering? Better just to say Johnny *has* cerebral palsy. Simple word changes equal big differences in perception.

- *Use* typical *or* regular *instead of* normal *when referring to children.* There really is no such thing as "normal." Most children have some kind of special need (as do most adults). Some needs are just more obvious. Don't point out individual differences if they're not relevant.

- *Use the word* challenges *instead of the word* problems *when referring to a child's needs.* This simple word shift may help change the way you view your demands, helping you work toward more *positive* solutions.

I can hear some of you saying (loudly) that words don't really matter, including some of you with special needs. In a perfect world, you'd be right. But we don't live in a perfect world and until we do (not likely), our language choices will continue to affect the lives of children with special needs—and our attitudes toward them.

Childhood labels can last a lifetime and may give others carte blanche to predetermine a child's abilities. That means some children may have serious strikes against them before they even get up to bat—all because someone has focused on the negative interpretations of words.

Words are mighty powerful! Be careful how you choose 'em and be careful how you use 'em . . .

Dealing with Staring

If there's one thing most families of children with special needs can agree on, it's this: staring stinks!!

No doubt about it, when people stare at our children (or us), they make us squirm. Let's face it, people rarely stare at us because they're mesmerized by our great beauty. More likely, they are sizing up our glaring imperfections. For kids with special needs, those imperfections may be hard to hide.

During an especially intense episode of staring, most of us (if we are really honest) have found ourselves thinking, "If only our looks back could kill . . . !"

It helps to learn how to deal with staring in a more productive and less stressful way, whether it occurs in the school hallways, at church or the zoo, at the movies, on vacation, or while you're buying ice cream and cereal and milk at the supermarket. You can't avoid staring in public.

For some families, this issue is so upsetting that it interferes with their freedom to move about in society like everybody else. That's why I'm challenging you to look at staring in a whole new way. Ask yourself this one question:

What if staring is actually a good thing? (Please don't throw things at me!) After more than a decade of returning not-so-friendly fire to people who stared at my son and me, here's my take on the subject: you never know *why* someone is staring. It may provide you with a rare, priceless opportunity to educate society about the value of your child and others with special needs. That's time well spent.

JUDY WINTER'S TIPS

Staring

Here are some valuable thoughts to help defuse all those uncomfortable feelings you may get when people stare at you and your child in public. When people stare, keep these possibilities in mind:

- *People think your child is cute.* That's not so bad. If I had a buck for every person who stopped us to say how cute and how adorable our son was, I would be one rich mama! Eric *was* cute.

- *They have a family member with special needs and feel a kinship with you.* Or they work with children with special needs and have a heartfelt story to share. That's not so painful either.

- *They are having difficulty dealing with special needs in their own lives.* Or they are new parents of a child with similar challenges and have questions, like what kind of wheelchair or stroller to buy. Share your expertise.

- *They have lost a child with special needs and seeing your child causes them to remember special outings with their own child.* That's how it is now for me. Try not to shut these families out. Offer them hugs, a shoulder, or tissues instead.

- *Children stare because they are curious.* Adults are a different story. My advice is to smile or wave at kids or ask if they have a question. Most will respond by smiling or waving back or asking a question—which gives you a great opportunity to tell them about special needs, before sending them off as little ambassadors to educate the adults in their lives (a much bigger task).

Staring is part of the deal that comes with giving your child every opportunity to be fully included in society. The good news is that it often gets easier to handle once you come to love and accept your child unconditionally. The next time someone stares at you or your child, give the benefit of the doubt—and think of it as an opportunity to enlighten this person.

Unless you prefer to stay home for the rest of your life.

SPECIAL TIPS

You have more parenting power than you may think! The following tips encourage you to watch your own language, challenge the language use of others, and learn from your child. Taking such action will help change your life—and that of your child!

- *Never forget that you are your child's first and best teacher.* The words you use to interact with your child can make a difference. You are responsible for the future of a child. Treat this sacred and amazing honor with the respect it deserves, by using language that helps your child celebrate his or her full value. Build children up, don't knock them down.

- *Look into your child's eyes.* The old saying is really true: eyes *are* the windows to our souls. You can often tell what's going on in the mind of a child with special needs by watching the eyes. Try to connect with your child in this powerful way, especially if speech delays are involved. Don't assume a child doesn't understand what's going on around her just because she has a certain diagnosis or label, or because of biases.

- *Remember that all children have gifts and talents, including yours.* Look beyond limiting labels and language to uncover and nurture a child's individual gifts, even when those around you appear blind or indifferent to your child's value.

- *Believe in your ability to parent a child with special needs well.* Yes, you *can* do this. Change your inner talk to more positive language that helps you succeed.

- *Watch your tongue.* Words have the power to lift us up or crush us. Don't use limiting language when speaking about your child, and don't allow others to use it in your child's presence.

- *Use proper terminology to address special needs.* And place such words *after* the child's name (for example, the *child with autism,* not *the autistic kid).* Words hurt. Be careful how you use them.

- *Speak to your child using age-appropriate language.* Don't use baby talk, unless you are talking to a baby! Read to your children. Put them in social settings, go to the park, the playground, and the zoo. Even a few minutes of these regular childhood activities may affect a child's overall development and help reduce touch and noise sensitivity. Start small if these activities are difficult for your child to tolerate.

- *Don't put professionals on pedestals.* None of us belong there. Professionals are human (just like us) and they make mistakes (just like us). Welcome their valuable expertise, but don't worship them. No one knows a child better than a loving, involved parent! You're responsible for a child 24/7, including weekends and holidays—for life. Professionals should be in awe of *you.*

- *Offer your child lots of reassuring hugs and kisses and say I love you often.* Sometimes it's nice just to forget about special needs and connect with your child parent-to-child. I'll always treasure the memory of my son's amazing hugs, which came late in life because of his delayed motor skills. They were the best hugs ever! Savor such priceless moments—they *will* fuel you on.

Special Resources

Here are a few more resources that can provide you with helpful information.

Organizations

- National Information Center for Children with Disabilities (NICHCY): www.nichcy.org. Helpful NICHCY publications include *A Parent's Guide to Accessing Programs for Infants, Toddlers, and Preschoolers with Disabilities*.
- The ARC of the United States. To find a local chapter, visit www.thearc.org.
- The National Down Syndrome Society: www.ndss.org.
- Spina Bifida Association of America (SBAA): www.sbaa.org.
- United Cerebral Palsy (UCP): www.ucp.org.
- Easter Seals, Inc.: www.easterseals.com.
- Carrie's Cards: www.carriescards.biz.
- VSA Arts: supports the arts and special needs: www.vsarts.org.

Books

- *Babies with Down Syndrome: A New Parent's Guide*, by Karen Stray-Gundersen.
- *Down Syndrome: A Promising Future, Together*, by Terry J. Hassold and David Patterson.
- *Extraordinary People with Disabilities*, by Deborah Kent and Kathryn A. Quinlan.
- *Reason for Hope: A Spiritual Journey*, by Jane Goodall.

Special Note

Children with special needs are not broken or defective. Don't try *to fix* them! Running from program to program looking for quick fixes for your child's special needs will only exhaust, disappoint, and frustrate you—and your child. When you find a good program, commit to it fully—for your child's sake. Work hard to accept your child for who he really is.

You should be feeling increasingly empowered in your role as the parent of a child with special needs. And you've got some great resources to boot. Let's move on to Chapters Four and Five and take a look at the importance of early intervention and the challenging preschool through college years. Take a deep breath. These years will seem less daunting once you've got a few more parenting tools in hand . . .

PART TWO

GUIDELINES FOR THE PRESCHOOL THROUGH COLLEGE YEARS

JUDY WINTER'S
SPECIAL NEEDS BILL OF RIGHTS
FOR PARENTS

You have the right to

- Be treated with dignity and respect
- Celebrate your child's birth
- Grieve the loss of a child without special needs
- Move about freely in society with your child
- View your child as a child first, not as a disability
- Be proud of your child's accomplishments
- Ask family members for support
- Be proud of your advocacy efforts
- Take time for yourself and to nurture other relationships
- Advocate for change that helps your child succeed, including access to a good education
- Ask tough questions, including *Why?*

4

THE PRE-K AND ELEMENTARY YEARS

Those who say it cannot be done should not interrupt the person doing it.

—Chinese Proverb

You are now entering one of the most challenging stages of your child's life, and yours—the school-aged years. There's plenty of ground to cover during these years, so I've addressed it in two parts. This chapter addresses early intervention, preschool, elementary school, special education law, and the Individualized Education Program (the dreaded IEP!).

Chapter Five will address middle school, junior high school, high school, *transition planning,* and a few strategies for preparing for college and the workplace.

There's also that sticky issue about learning how to let go of your child so he or she can become a tad more independent. It's time to take another *deep breath.*

Few topics create such fear and apprehension in the minds of families with special needs children as education—and with good reason. The education system in this country can be intimidating, difficult, overwhelming, and maddeningly tough to navigate for these families. And you're being asked to entrust it with life decisions for a child for whom you feel very protective. You can help defuse these emotional issues through your parenting actions.

Despite its lofty and noble mission to educate all children, the education system in this country is at times ill prepared to deal with the demands of all children with special needs. Fortunately, many people within and without its ranks are working harder than ever these days to better meet these needs—and the federal mandates and special education guidelines that fuel them. Be aware that these efforts come at a time when ever-deeper budget cuts and inadequate federal and state funding for schools and community-based programs loom large across the country—a major economic problem that isn't going away any time soon. That makes things more challenging for you, but not impossible. With family and professional support, great resources, parent-to-parent networking, and *Breakthrough Parenting for Children with Special Needs*, you can handle whatever comes your way.

Don't be afraid to ask for help (again), and stay focused on your child! When it comes to the school years, three simple words rule: *knowledge is power*. So take full advantage of all the great special resources listed on pages 95–98. They will help you survive this demanding stage.

Before we get started on the heavier stuff, let's have some fun by sharing the life story of one of the most determined and engaging men I have ever met. This successful, children's-book author with cerebral palsy is someone you won't soon forget.

A SUCCESS STORY

Johnnie Tuitel is a charismatic speaker with a streetwise edge. The successful children's-book author has single-handedly dashed many familiar stereotypes about what people with special needs can't do—like graduating from high school and college, getting married, having three children, and becoming a successful author, businessman, and motivational speaker.

Tuitel is a wheelchair user and one of approximately 750,000 Americans with cerebral palsy (CP). According to Dr. Carl Gunderson, deputy director of the United Cerebral Palsy (UCP) Research and Educational Foundation, "Cerebral Palsy describes a group of developmental disorders of movement and posture, causing activity restriction or disability that are attributed to nonprogressive disturbances occurring in the fetal or infant brain."

Gunderson further states that cerebral palsy may also be accompanied by disturbances of sensation, cognition, and communication, as well as behavior and seizure disorders. It occurs in two to three out of a thousand live births in the United States. The life expectancy of those with CP depends on the degree and type of disability.

"Many with CP will have life expectancies within the normal range," Gunderson says. "Others with severe disabilities will die younger." In simple words, the physical and cognitive manifestations of CP range from mild to severe and encompass a wide range of challenges—from walking with a slight limp to having difficulty swallowing, to being unable to speak or walk. Gunderson says a few secondary conditions like arthritis and seizures may not manifest themselves for years.

Johnnie Tuitel entered the world forty-one years ago. He was born to Dutch immigrant parents, who never doubted his value. He was born three and a half months premature, after his mother's appendix ruptured. He weighed just one pound, four ounces and wasn't expected to live. His mother called him her *miracle baby*. "My mother used to say to me, 'I love you. You are fantastic and you are my son. And disabled or not, one day you are going to change the world.'"

Tuitel became one of the first students legally mainstreamed in Michigan, graduated from East Grand Rapids High School, and received a bachelor of arts degree in education from Hope College, a private liberal arts college in Holland, Michigan.

He was awarded the school's 2003 Distinguished Alumni Award—not too shabby, huh?

"We know several adults with cerebral palsy who hold senior corporate management positions and senior faculty positions at universities," Dr. Gunderson says, of expectations for those with CP. "The outlook for individuals with CP is dependent upon their unique condition."

Tuitel credits loving, supportive parents with much of his success, but his toughest moments also shaped him. "I wore one pair of shoes—those *Forest Gump* boots," Tuitel says. "His braces ran up his legs, but mine went all the way up to my chest." His parents were told he would never go to a regular school, and when the armchair jock realized he couldn't play football exactly like other guys, it hit him hard.

With clear speech, a captivating grin, and infectious charisma, Tuitel still wheeled himself to impressive life success—including regular speaking engagements across the country, where he bulldozes his way past the term *disabled* with his quick wit and ability to laugh at his challenges.

"Just for the irony of it, I'm wearing walking shoes today," he says. "I bought 'em, thinking they'd help. But they don't work. I put them on and fell flat on my face!"

Tuitel encourages others to pursue personal success. "Then give something back to the world," he challenges. "Because when you take the focus off yourself and put it where it belongs—it changes your life forever."

Giving back is at the cornerstone of Tuitel's life. In 1994, he and his business partner and friend, George Ranville, created Alternatives in Motion, a nonprofit corporation providing wheelchairs to those who can't afford them. The organization was born of Tuitel's outrage at being denied a new wheelchair by his insurance company, following corrective back surgery.

As of June 2005, Alternatives in Motion has provided more than six hundred wheelchairs to those in need. The organization currently serves the United States but will network with organizations answering the call for chairs internationally.

Working with coauthor, Sharon Lamson, and partner, George Ranville, Tuitel is also the author of six adventure books, entitled the *Gunn Lake Adventure Series*. Like Tuitel, the books' hero has CP and uses a wheelchair.

Renaissance Learning, a leading program for enhancing math, writing, and reading skills, recently picked up the series' first five books as part of their Accelerated Reader Program, used by over sixty thousand schools in the United States.

Did I mention that Johnnie's been married to Deb for fifteen years and has three healthy sons: Nick, age eleven, PJ, age eight, and Joel, who's six?

Tuitel's life is a model of possibilities. He hates being called inspirational, but that's how many people view him. "Forty years ago, my parents were advised to begin planning my funeral because I wasn't supposed to live," he explains. "But my mom said, 'No way! We're going to see how this story ends!'

"And folks, it's not over yet."

Today Johnnie Tuitel's life has solid purpose and meaning, in large part due to his parents' great love—and some good educational opportunities from an early age. Let's see how you can realize positive educational outcomes for your child—but first, you need to know something about the law.

UNDERSTANDING THE LAW

Before we continue, you need to have at least a brief understanding of the laws backing your child's right to pursue a good public education. Unless otherwise stated, the source for the following legal information section is Wrightslaw (www.wrightslaw.com), and *From Emotions to Advocacy: The Special Education Survival Guide* by Pam Wright and Pete Wright.

• The *Individuals with Disabilities Education Act (IDEA)* is a federal law enacted by Congress in 1975 to provide children with special needs guaranteed access to a free and appropriate public education. (It was formerly known as the Education for All Handicapped Children Act of 1975.) IDEA requires states to first identify and assess children with special needs (defined as *child find*), then provide them with the necessary services and programs to help them succeed. IDEA was reauthorized with changes in 1997—and again in 2004 with the Improving Education Results for Children with Disabilities Act. It was recognized that having special needs doesn't mean something is *wrong* with your child. It means he requires assistance to meet educational goals and transition to adult life—*so what?* There's nothing wrong with that! Prior to IDEA, children with disabilities could be denied access to public education. They were either ignored or sent to less-than-stellar programs. Many children were institutionalized. We have come a long way, baby. But we've got miles to walk.

• *Section 504 of the Rehabilitation Act* of 1973 in part prohibits discrimination against individuals with disabilities (in buildings and activities funded by federal subsidies and grants) and ensures equal access to education.

• *The No Child Left Behind Act (NCLBA)* of 2002 was designed to improve academic achievement for all students, including those with special needs. It holds schools accountable for such achievement. NCLBA is based on stronger accountability for results, more freedom for states and communities (flexibility in use of federal education funds), proven education methods, and more choices for parents (options to transfer students to better-performing schools). The NCLBA mandates reasonable adaptations and accommodations for students with disabilities (under IDEA) to help level the playing field for *all* kids. (*Source:* U.S. Department of Education/ed.gov.)

NCLBA is not without serious criticism. In short, NCLBA is highly controversial, and many states and school districts are now refusing to comply or are resisting it in the courts. Who knows where it will stand by the time you read this book. When I speak to educators and future educators, I am almost always asked my take on this law. Here it is: I believe that the *mission* of NCLBA—to close the educational achievement gap among all students—is a noble one and long overdue and one I strongly support.

That said, I believe such important legislation must also be backed by the professional training, additional classroom staff, and resources, including financial, that are required for it to succeed—things not yet in place. The reality is that no one law will instantly solve all the ills existing from years of exclusion and deeply rooted stereotypes.

Although flawed, NCLBA mandates represent an important start, but it is my sincere hope that we will continue to build solidly on what this law represents: educational equality for all. In the meantime, determined parental advocacy efforts on behalf of our children will continue to reign supreme.

IDEA is the centerpiece of all the legislation pertaining to a child's right to access a free public education. It's really important that you have a firm grasp of it so you can knowledgeably advocate for your child's rights. So here's the *"Reader's Digest"* version of IDEA:

- It's a federal law protecting the educational rights of kids with special needs.

- *Special education* is the term for that part of the educational system that addresses and meets the educational needs of children with special needs, once they're determined eligible.

- The Individualized Education Program (IEP) is at the core of IDEA.

- IDEA was reauthorized in 2004.

- The law mandates that states identify and assess children with special needs and provide them with appropriate services and programs to help them achieve educational success.

- The rights and procedures addressed under IDEA cover ages birth through twenty-six.

- By age sixteen, *transition planning and services* to help prepare your child for life after high school must be addressed in the IEP. (There's more about *transition* on pages 111–112.)

- IDEA entitles your child to a *free and appropriate public education* (FAPE), designed to meet *your* child's needs (through the IEP).

- IDEA grants your child the right to be educated in the *least restrictive environment* (LRE), often referred to as *mainstreaming*, or, increasingly, *inclusion*. The ideal result of LRE is having a child educated in a general education classroom along with students without special needs. It can be the subject of much-heated debate!

That's a *brief* look at IDEA—now let's see how it works.

Accessing Early Intervention

If ever there was a buzzword in the world of parenting young children, it's *early intervention*—also known as *early on, early prevention, ages 0–3*, the *wonder years*, and other terms probably coined after this book went to press.

Brenda Lou Turner has been a registered occupational therapist (OTR) for twenty-four years and an early on services coordinator in Michigan since 1989. She was one of my first professional contacts after my son was diagnosed with CP at birth. When Eric came home, I had no intention of opening my door to any professional, no matter how nice. I was still in denial about my parenting situation—I just wanted Brenda Lou to *go away* forever. Sound familiar? But this skilled and gently persistent OTR stuck with me until I finally let her in the door—for Eric's sake. It was one of the best decisions I have ever made.

There are few professionals for whom I have such respect. Turner explains that early intervention is the name for the federally mandated program for identifying and serving children birth through age three. It falls under Section C of IDEA. Early intervention is a joint effort involving community and statewide agencies, such as mental health, social services, and education. Contacts and programs vary, but all states must provide early intervention programs and services to children who qualify. You can connect with your own state program by using the information under Special Resources listed on page 96.

Think of early intervention as an umbrella designed to protect your child from potentially stormy developmental seas. The big part of the umbrella is IDEA. It protects children with a federally mandated early intervention system—a plan of action by all states. Got it? Under that big umbrella are *all the agencies* in your county or state that are holding it up. They work together providing your child with services and support to affect growth and learning. Still with me? Under those agencies and services, subcategories help protect your child from future developmental storms. These programs and services help children once they reach age three by transitioning them to *special education*. That's it!

How to Qualify for Early Intervention Programs and Services

Early intervention helps all kids have better life starts. Turner explains briefly how your child qualifies. Check your state's guidelines. (*Source:* Early On Michigan, www.cenmi.org.)

- Infants are assessed at birth in the hospital by qualified professionals for risk factors associated with developmental delays, using indicators like prematurity, low birth weight, and Apgar scores, the first assessment of a newborn used to determine the infant's physical health and well-being, plus any additional need for immediate medical intervention or treatment.

- If risk factors are indicated, a referral is made to an early intervention program or another appropriate link in that county—with a parent's signed permission for release of information.

- The referral is followed by a home visit, and an assessment is done, including a health assessment, parent-child observation, family questionnaire, and a developmental evaluation of your child.

- Eligibility for services is determined based on one of two factors: your child has either an established condition *or* a developmental delay.

- An Individualized Family Service Plan (IFSP) is created. Turner explains that this plan of action includes your child's health-care team, your family strengths and concerns, your child's strengths and concerns, and outcome and goals based on your family's input.

If you are concerned about your child's development, you should contact your child's physician or your state's early intervention coordinator to begin the process of having your child assessed. Don't be shy about voicing your concerns. Far better to address this early than to lose valuable intervention time. "If nothing else, you'll get a child's baseline for comparison for concerns down the road," Turner says. "We're getting to children earlier than ever before and that's good, because the sooner we get to them, the better the outcomes." There's your permission to act right now! In case you felt you needed it.

Turner says the biggest change in early intervention over the past few years has been that everything is now family centered. "It's strength based," she continues. "Everything used to be focused on what are the deficiencies of a child and family. Now the focus is on a child's strengths and how to support families, because if we support families, we support the child."

That's a huge shift in thinking from when I started this journey, and it indicates a long overdue respect for the important role parents play. "Parents are key," Turner stresses. "They are their child's most important teacher and best advocate," she says. "Professionals come and go, but parents are there for the long haul."

Now consider yourself valued and validated—and get to work. Remember—you cannot get these developmental years back!

For many families, this parenting push may come while they're still struggling with the reality of having a child with special needs. So how the heck are they supposed to jump on the early intervention bandwagon?

Just do it! If your child is receiving services, you've already got team members on board that bring valuable resources, insight, and experiences to help your child succeed. Pick their brains. This is the beginning of that all-important family and professional *teamwork*. Make good use of it.

Picking the Best Program for Your Child

When looking for a program for your child, here's my advice:

- Look for dynamic programs that best meet your child's individual needs. If you're uncomfortable with a program or professional, make a change. It *can* make a difference.

- Seek out family-friendly programs focused on a child's ability and on helping the child achieve maximum independence. Put the child first. Always.

- Commit to good programs. If a program fits your child's needs, commit to it long term. Some gains take time. Be patient.

- Be prepared to pay for cutting-edge programs yourself. Insurance and other programs may not cover such costs.

UNDERSTANDING THE INDIVIDUALIZED EDUCATION PROGRAM

Few letters of the alphabet strike fear in the hearts of parents of children with special needs as much as the letters **I, E,** and **P.** Stand them alone and they could be the letters of the day on *Sesame Street.* But knit 'em together and you get IEP, or an Individualized Educational Program, the result of the annual meeting between professionals and parents of school-aged children with special needs. It's not that scary—*if* you're prepared.

According to the U.S. Department of Education's *Guide to the Individualized Education Program* (available on its Web site: www.ed.gov), every child receiving special education and related services must have an IEP.

In a nutshell, an IEP is a working document drafted by a team in a meeting including parents, usually held once a year, to create and implement a child's educational program—including goals and objectives, placement, and related services that meet *your* child's public education needs, like occupational, speech, and physical therapy, and counseling. An IEP can be called anytime.

Many parents define an IEP as a dreaded yearly event where professionals tell them, often arrogantly, exactly what's wrong with their child, instead of what's right. Some educators view these meetings as the time of year when parents make unyielding and unrealistic demands of schools.

I still remember my son's first IEP (it wasn't the least bit fun). I sat in a stuffy room, outnumbered by those citing expertise about children. I talked too fast, trying to share good stuff about Eric. His potential was never mentioned, except by me.

With the exception of facing my son's death, participating in these meetings was the toughest thing I've ever done in my life. Lucky for you, times are slowly changing.

As parents become increasingly empowered and demand more of the system, and education increasingly focuses on strength-based decisions, ensuring good outcomes for *all* children, the IEP process is becoming more user friendly and successful for all parties.

Alleluia!

That said, your attitude, actions, and preparation *will* help determine how positive and productive your IEP experience is. Be proactive and prepare well!

Nuts and Bolts of the Individualized Education Program

The IEP is the crown jewel (centerpiece) of IDEA. Children must be found eligible for special education to have an IEP—which means having a disability that interferes with their education. Here's how it goes:

- Your child's first IEP team meeting must be held or written within thirty days after your child qualifies for special education.

- Parents are considered *partners* in this process. An IEP team consists of parents, teachers (general or special education— or both), qualified school district personnel, and other professionals responsible for planning and implementing your child's education goals, objectives, and related services.

- The IEP team's focus must be on creating a program that best meets *your* child's needs, not the school's or another child's— that's what *individualized* means, and the school *must* keep you informed about how your child is doing.

- By at least age sixteen, the IEP must address transition planning and transition services to help your child prepare for life after high school. See Transition on page 111.

- During the IEP, a formal document is written, stating the goals and objectives (how much, how often, by whom?) and classroom placement (LRE) for your child. Be careful crafting this document! It will be the plan of action for your child's school year. If you don't agree, speak up. If it's not in the IEP, there's a really good chance it won't happen.

Note: You do not have to sign the IEP in the meeting. You may take it home for further review, which I highly recommend. But make sure you understand *when it must be finalized* with the school.

Realizing Success with an IEP

Eric's IEPs became increasingly positive when our skilled team focused on celebrating his accomplishments and strengths *first*, and then addressing challenges creatively. This dynamic approach requires unified teamwork, mutual respect, and participants who are willing to share important information.

I suggest you attend your child's IEP meeting well prepared (it pays to review your child's school file), head held high with a sense of humor intact—and your child's value and face clearly imprinted in your mind. An IEP is nothing more than a meeting, although a pretty important one.

Most parents have already faced far worse stuff and have survived. Remember the initial diagnosis?

JUDY WINTER'S TIPS
Surviving the IEP

Follow these tips and you may just get the results you want and need for your child's IEP success:

- *Be prepared.* Think Boy Scouts. Come armed with knowledge about the laws and about the services to which your child is entitled. Celebrate your child's strengths and address challenges. Don't pretend that your child doesn't have any! I prepared user-friendly packets with important information about my son and included his photograph, recent reports, and our goals for him, which I gave to everyone. Help professionals know your child *beyond* a diagnosis.

- *Ask questions—lots of them.* This is a legally binding document for which team members are held accountable. Don't be intimidated.

- *Watch your language.* And bite your tongue, too! Don't apologize for your child's needs. Children with special needs (people-first language) have a right to services that help them reach their full potential, just like other children. Avoid using words that are combative or threatening. They rarely solve anything. Dress professionally; it can help gain you more respect.

- *Conduct yourself with class, confidence, and dignity.* Such actions will earn you greater respect, which is especially important when first meeting your child's team, where everyone's sizing up the situation. Be confident. Be a good communicator. And be an even better listener. Try to listen more than you talk. (We all struggle with this one.) Express gratitude for the role that each of these individuals plays in your child's successes.

- *State your goals for your child clearly.* First, decide what
  they are: Do you want your child to graduate high
  school? Take music classes? Ride a regular school bus? Be
  part of after-school activities? Who will supervise? How
  will the team make these things happen? When you dis-
  agree, do it in a way that is respectful, even when you are
  angry. But don't roll over and play dead. Good communication helps avoid costly and draining litigation. Keep
  the energy level up, but be careful about too much caffeine and too many doughnuts! Take a healthy snack or
  beverages to the IEP. Team meetings are often held when
  energy is running low and emotions high. A healthy
  energy boost can help you maintain your cool and your
  focus. Humanize the process whenever possible.

- *Don't forget to laugh—so you don't cry.* Interject appropriate humor into the IEP. I once gave everyone colorful
  plastic sunglasses to put on. It broke the ice! I'm sure
  they were talking about me afterward, but they didn't forget me. We think we need to be stoic and demanding or
  cite credentials to get what we need or to save face. That
  unyielding approach makes these meetings nasty. You
  can get better results for less grief by flashing a few smiles.

- *Have your child participate in the IEP process.* Your child
  has a right to be included in this meeting—it's the
  child's life, *after all.* Your child's presence can help keep
  the focus where it belongs, while encouraging everybody to think carefully about their behavior. Invite
  additional team support. Bring in the *big* guns. If you're
  concerned about standing face-to-face with others in
  this meeting or expect resistance, even hostility, from
  your district, you have the right to have an attorney or
  child advocate present, and you may bring someone to

(continued on next page)

(continued from previous page)

take notes (highly recommended) or tape the meeting. Notify the school of your plans in advance. It's a smart move.

- *Don't be starstruck.* This definitely ain't Hollywood, folks. Don't be intimidated by all the credentials flying around the room. Can these people suction a trache, clean a feeding tube, give injections and breathing treatments—all in twenty-four hours? The wealth of knowledge that parents share regarding their children helps educators be more successful at what they do, which is to teach our kids.

- *Share the spotlight.* It's time to model cohesive partnerships. At these meetings, each parent's voice should be heard—*if* more than one is involved. Prepare ahead of time and decide who's addressing what, to ensure that all voices are heard and respected.

- *Remember my definition of an IEP?*—Increasingly empowered (and effective) parent. These three powerful words can change your perception of this process—and help prevent more gray hairs.

- *Don't even think about skipping your child's IEP!* Participate!

Now let's go through your child's educational ages and stages, step-by-step. This discussion will continue in Chapter Five.

Preschool

When your child reaches age three, he or she will transition from early intervention to special education services (Part B of IDEA), a process that begins about six months earlier. If your child is already part of early intervention, your current team members can help walk you through this. Other families should contact their school districts or state agencies for information on programs and services.

I love this age! It's a time of childhood innocence, untapped potential, brain development, and if you're lucky, lots of hugs and kisses. It's also a great time to address such issues as socialization, friendship, and discipline.

Some of these Pre-K tips will prove useful throughout your child's life:

- *Enroll your child in a regular preschool.* It can be hard work to realize this goal, but it's worth it. The social gains made by a child in these settings can help create a firm foundation for future learning and sociability. My son attended regular preschool for two years. It made a huge difference in his ability to succeed in an inclusive educational setting later on. Aim high! Let your child go! I know it's tough, but your child needs to begin claiming some independence, however small. That fuels the independence and confidence necessary for future life success.

- *Discipline your child appropriately.* Far too many adults use special needs as an excuse to allow inappropriate behavior. I've never forgotten the words of a physical therapist, who told me that she believed nothing was worse than a child with special needs who is spoiled or lacking in discipline. She was right. We worked hard to hold our son to much the same discipline as his sister, so he could move about in the world successfully, too. The challenge is to sort out what behavior is a result of your child's needs and what is the result of parenting. Talk with your physician or parents of similarly challenged children to get their suggestions, but don't ignore this. All parents have a responsibility to address discipline. It's part of raising a healthy, productive child.

- *Good grooming is also important to your child.* It helps children fit in and may help others feel more comfortable around them.

- *Consider joining a parent group*. Choose wisely. Avoid pity parties, combative behaviors, and threats of litigation, loudly proclaimed as diehard solutions. Such encounters will leave you with little more than a really bad migraine headache.

Time now for another big transition—kindergarten. Alert the presses, get the camera and camcorder ready. Your baby is finally going to school.

K Through Elementary Years

These school years will be driven by your child's annual IEP—and—again—some of these tips on public education may prove useful for years to come.

- *Push for regular classroom settings*. Inclusion means *being included* whenever possible—just like other students. The law, research, and my own experiences back this push.
- *Focus on your child's ability*. And ask other to do the same. Put what you've learned about language and limiting labels into action.
- *Explore the use of state-of-the-art technology for your child*. This is especially helpful for a child with speech or motor challenges. It can be crucial to educational success, assessments, and participating in grade-level academics. The Assistive Technology Act of 2004 supports this.
- *Address teasing and bullying*. Children with special needs are at increased risk for teasing and bullying. If this is happening to your child, take action to stop it now.
- *Visit your child's class*. Let all the kids ask all their questions. And take treats. When you educate them, they educate others. It's amazing.
- *Make careful, thoughtful decisions about the classroom teacher and about placements*. My experiences tell me that it does *too* matter! Don't let anyone tell you otherwise.

- *Know your child's bus driver.* And make sure your child gets to school on time. It's your responsibility to make sure your child is ready for school when the bus comes. Please don't be late. It's not fair to your child or to other kids on the bus.

- *Continue good grooming.* Get your child a good haircut and some stylish back-to-school clothing. If budget is a concern, shop garage sales in upscale neighborhoods or discount stores. These things help children fit in more easily. Yes, it *does* matter.

- *Invite kids over to play.* If you wait for someone else to invite your child over to play, it may not happen. Sorry, but it's true.

- *Make sure that your child is included in classroom testing and assessments whenever possible.* Accommodations must be provided for your child. No child should be left out of regular classroom activities and learning.

- *Involve your child in after-school activities whenever possible.* Such activities enhance socialization and help foster acceptance, friendship, and inclusion. Opportunities also exist for kids to take part in such activities as swimming, dance, art, music, drama, and sports if traditional classes and environments are tough for them.

SPECIAL TIPS

Funding is one of the most critical issues facing special needs families today. Because I find it so critical for families to get involved in funding issues and education, I've made it the *only* Special Tip for this chapter.

- *Make some noise! Parent power* really does help create much-needed change. Don't just whine about the lack of services and programs in your district and state or threaten litigation. Help *change* it. I know you're busy, but you can take time to write an important letter regarding funding and mail it to statewide and national politicians. And yes, to the president

DID YOU KNOW?

According to the National Center for Learning Disabilities Web site (www.ld.org), in 2004 nearly 2.9 million school-aged children in the United States had *specific learning disabilities* (SLD). That's how prevalent they are. A *learning disability* (LD) doesn't make your child less intelligent or less valued than other children. It means we need to uncover how their brains learn best and support that learning style. A friend once told me about a great billboard about LD that she saw. It proclaimed, *don't dis our kids*.

There's nothing wrong with having an LD—or with your child! (Think Tom Cruise and Cher.) But you must take action to help your child succeed—and help reduce the dropout and retention rates, and shame, of having an LD.

of the United States. Families must unite and work toward resolutions for serious funding issues affecting their children's lives. No one cares as much as you do about effecting positive change (not even me!). *The bold actions of one person can make a difference.*

Special Note

Some people argue that we should refrain from portraying those with special needs as *heroes* for fear of building false expectations in families. I beg to differ. The word *hero* also stands for perseverance and success against all the odds. That fuels possibilities, motivation, and hope. The accomplishments of those with special needs have been shamefully left out of history. Did you know that former president Franklin Delano Roosevelt was expected to hide his wheelchair use?

Think of all the awareness that might have been created had his needs been made public. Think Christopher Reeve. More about this super man in Chapter Ten.

Most children grow up idolizing heroes—it's part of our life experience. Many of us may not achieve the success of our idols, but we manage to go on with our lives. So can kids with special needs. The people in this book have earned our credos. They *are* our heroes. Embrace them.

Special Resources

There are so many great resources online today. Here's a few to get you started. Most offer many other valuable resource links.

Organizations

- United Cerebral Palsy (UCP): www.ucp.org.

- Children and Adults with Attention-Deficit/Hyperactivity Disorder (ADHD) (CHADD): www.chadd.org.

- National Center for Learning Disabilities (NCLD): www.ld.org.

- National Alliance for the Mentally Ill: www.nami.org. Help Line: 1-800-950-NAMI.

- National Black Child Development Institute: www.nbcbi.org.

- TASH: Equity, Diversity, Social Justice, and Inclusion for those with severe special needs, who are most at risk of societal exclusion: www.tash.org. TASH features information on Breaking the Barriers, a national effort to ensure the right to communication for those with special needs.

- Johnnie Tuitel: Alternatives in Motion (wheelchairs)/ *Gunn Lake Adventure Series*, motivational speaker: www.tapshoe.com.

Assessment

- *Assessing Infants and Preschoolers with Special Needs*, by Mary McLean, Mark Wolery, and Donald B. Bailey.

- *Assessing Students with Special Needs*, by James A. McLoughlin.

Early Intervention

- National Early Childhood Technical Assistance Center (NECTAC): information on IDEA and programs like early intervention programs for infants and toddlers with disabilities and statewide links for early intervention programs. www.nectac.org.

- Social Security Online: www.ssa.gov.

- National Library of Medicine (NLM): www.nlm.nih.gov.

- Parents Action for Children: www.iamyourchild.org.

- Zero to Three: www.zerotothree.org.

- Parent Advocacy Coalition for Educational Rights (PACER): www.pacer.org: great links and programs, including for grandparents.

- *The Black Parenting Book*, by Allison Abner, Linda Villarosa, and Anne C. Beal.

The Individualized Education Program (IEP)

- U.S. Department of Education (USDE): www.ed.gov: offers many good publications (ED Pubs), including the *Guide to the Individualized Education Program* and *Students with Disabilities: Preparing for Postsecondary Education: Know Your Rights and Responsibilities*.

- The Council for Exceptional Children (CEC): www.cec.sped.org. Includes information on the Yes I Can!

Foundation for Exceptional Children (focused on potential): www.yesican.cec.sped.org.

- Attainment Company (IEP Resources): www.Attainment Company.com.

Inclusion

- The Inclusion Web site: http://inclusion.ngfl.gov.uk.
- FAPE, helping adults improve educational results for children with special needs: www.FAPE.org.
- Wiley Publishers: www.wiley.com: offers the Wiley higher education link for creating partnerships with professionals.
- www.allkindsofminds.org: featuring parent/professional resources and the best-selling works of Dr. Mel Levine: *Ready or Not Here Life Comes* (school-to-work transition), *The Myth of Laziness*, and *A Mind at a Time*.
- Easter Seals: www.easterseals.com: Friends Who Care— resources for families/professionals to foster positive attitudes of disability in schools.
- *How the Special Needs Brain Learns*, by David A. Sousa.
- *Inclusion: 450 Strategies for Success: A Practical Guide for All Educators Who Teach Students with Disabilities*, by Peggy A. Hammeken.
- *Inclusion: A Practical Guide for Parents: Tools to Enhance Your Child's Success in Learning*, by Lorraine O. Moore, Ph.D.
- *Delicate Threads: Friendships Between Children with and Without Special Needs in Inclusive Settings*, by Debbie Staub, Ph.D. (states benefits/researched based).

The Law

- U.S. Department of Education (USDE): www.ed.gov: for information on all laws related to education and special needs.

- U.S. Department of Justice, ADA home page: www.ada.gov.
- National Coalition for Disability Rights (NCDR): www.ADAWatch.org.
- The National Disability Party: www.disabilityparty.com.
- SchwabLearning.org and the National Center for Learning Disabilities (NCLD) have developed the handbook *Making the "No Child Left Behind Act" Work for Children Who Struggle to Learn: A Parent's Guide*.
- Wrightslaw: www.wrightslaw.com: special education law and advocacy.

Are you doing OK so far with this school discussion? Hope so, because in Chapter Five, we're going to pick up the educational pace and address the educational needs of adolescents, teens, and young adults. Are you ready?

5

MIDDLE SCHOOL, JUNIOR HIGH, AND HIGH SCHOOL

When I look at a child he inspires in me two sentiments: tenderness for what he is and respect for what he may become.
—Louis Pasteur

The second part of our discussion of the school-aged years raises the educational stakes, so we need to up our parenting game. Because the discussion of education has been divided into two chapters, there are no new Special Tips, Special Note, or Success Story in this chapter—just in case you're wondering. But I've got another great story for you in Chapter Six.

THEY AREN'T BABIES ANYMORE

For now, let's continue where we left off—by focusing our attention on those challenging (and emotional) adolescent, teen, and young adult years.

Middle School, Junior High, and High School Years

These are challenging years for children *without* special needs, so imagine what they're like for children who struggle? (It's not easy.) During the middle school, junior high, and high school years, children face issues of dating, sexuality, increasing independence, graduation, preparing for college and the workplace—we can't cover all that here. So check out the resources on pages 109–110 and 118–121, and do your homework.

My Son's Education Journey Ends— Yours Continues On

Because my son's life ended abruptly at age twelve, while in sixth grade, this is a bittersweet stage for me. Even though many challenges still lay ahead for my son, we were excited about forging important new educational ground together. Instead, I've committed myself to helping you walk this road well—I know that is what Eric would want.

Your actions during the adolescent and young adult years are especially critical. Unfortunately, many families become so stressed by the demands of this stage, and the professional resistance they've faced, that they may take their children out of inclusive settings (if they ever placed them there) and put them in centered-based programs and restricted classrooms—or let them drop out. Please explore every other possibility for your child first. Don't just take an easy way out. It can be tough to advocate for societal inclusion. But your child deserves the life opportunities that may come with such determined efforts. For some families, their expectations of their children may now be seriously altered. They may be burned out, disillusioned, or just plain sick and tired of the battles. I support families in making decisions that are right for their own particular situations, but there is always a price to pay. In many school districts, much-needed inclusive programs are still not in place for many teens and young adults, and many IEP teams are still unfamiliar with how to successfully make inclusion work during these years. Worst of all, some children may be leading less-fulfilling and less-productive lives and achieving less than they might have. Sadly, too many children end up in our juvenile justice system. Our parenting decisions can have serious rippling effects. *Someone* must help break through this developmental wasteland.

I hope that by using this book and all the great resources it provides, that someone is *you*. Many things make these years challenging. So not only must you meet the daily demands of your child's needs but you also, like most parents, are now being assaulted at every turn by all that other nerve-wracking developmental stuff: like growing independence, puberty, cliques, risky behaviors and sexuality, driving, and other increasing social and academic expectations. Plus, your children are supposed to be getting a good education that helps prepare them for college and work and becoming productive adults and model citizens. It's a potential parenting minefield. Tread carefully. Let's defuse it a bit by sharing some strategies for the preteen, teen, and young adult years.

Key Issues Facing Middle School Students

These years represent the final stronghold of childhood innocence, a time when the main focus of school is still on learning, and most kids are pretty accepting of differences. But as societal and family issues have become increasingly complex for even the youngest students, so have the issues they face in school, like dealing with bullying and teasing, building friendships, developing self-esteem, and wanting more independence. Having special needs often complicates these issues. Here are a few strategies to help you through these middle years:

• *Address bullying and teasing.* Research indicates that children with special needs are at greater risk of being teased and bullied. This is the age when differences in physical appearances and behaviors *do* matter. It's at this age that cliques begin to form, and those with special needs may be singled out as being different. Here's what you can do: teach your child to ask for help when it's needed: empower them! They need to know that teasing and bullying are not OK, and they need to know what actions they can take to address them. If your child's safety is at risk, get involved *now*. Don't blame the victim! At this age, if it's bad enough for them to tell you about it, it's probably pretty unbearable. Don't buy the argument that "it's just kids being kids." Kids aren't born mean spirited. Adults need to *teach* them that this behavior is not acceptable and won't be tolerated.

• *Keep in regular touch with the counseling staff.* These years keep school counselors busy. Network with staff on a regular basis to see how your child is adjusting to the school setting and socializing with other students. Address any of your concerns, and include your child in these discussions.

• *Encourage friendships.* This is important to your child's development as a healthy, well-adjusted adolescent. Do everything you can to make your child feel included and valued. Children need to feel that *they* belong, too. Help initiate and arrange social outings whenever you can. If you wait for others to invite your child to participate in social activities, you may be sorely disappointed. This may well be one more role you must take on to ensure your child has a full life. Invite kids to go bowling or to the movies. Let your house be the safe, welcoming place where kids hang out. The alternative may be lonely, isolated nights at home for your child; that's not a good thing. Encourage involvement in and attendance at important school events, like dances, sporting activities, yearbook, school plays, and others. Involvement in activities further fuels your child's sense of belonging and acceptance—in the world and with his peers. Plus they're fun! These things build the *whole* child and foster dreams. Encourage your child to try out for the school play or band and then help make it happen. Include professionals in addressing any concerns regarding full participation.

• *Maintain a line of open communication with your child.* Open, honest communication is critical. Children need to be told what's *right* with them. They already hear way too much about what's wrong with them. Allow them to express their feelings about special needs. And don't censor them. Encourage journal writing and seek out appropriate support. Let their voices be heard, too.

• *Feed your child's self-esteem.* Children need to know how much they're loved, valued, and respected. They need to see and understand their value beyond disability. My son and I discussed issues like teasing and staring and how it affected him. I assured him that nothing was wrong with *him*. I told him he was a teacher creating much-needed and important awareness about differences. That role made him proud and helped him handle some tough social and academic moments well. He knew his real value and importance in life. He knew he was more than just a disability and that helped fuel his confidence and motivation.

- *Respect growing independence.* Like all children, your son or daughter is growing increasingly independent, something especially critical for kids with special needs. Fuel this independence in productive, nurturing, age-appropriate ways and address important needs, like medical concerns. Don't deny your child an opportunity for independence because of *your* limited perceptions of a disability—or because you want to protect her (or yourself) from more pain or suffering. If you are limiting her life experiences without good reason, that's not OK. Don't baby your children. They aren't babies anymore. My son had significant physical and speech needs, but we balanced his needs with rewarding life experiences. We took risks and it was worth it!

- *Don't do your child's homework for her.* Work alongside her, guide her, and offer support where needed (and when requested), but make sure it is as much her own work as possible. Be prepared to document the details of such assistance for teachers, who may question who *really* did the work. If your child needs assistance because of challenged motor skills, discuss accommodations and adaptations with the IEP team. If your child needs tutoring or technology, seek them out. Don't just do things to her or for her. Let your child show you what she *can* do. Don't leave homework until the last minute or until late at night.

- *Encourage your child to be part of important decisions about his life.* Allow him to choose his own clothes, hairstyle, activities, and friends (but pay attention to this). Allow your child to do things for himself whenever possible. Don't disable him further. Enable him!

- *Respect your child's growing need for privacy.* Give 'em some space. Children with special needs often have many people involved in making decisions about their lives, which makes it tough for them to hear their own voices and recognize their own dreams. Like adults, they need time alone to regroup and dream. Allow it. Honor That Privacy. Whether it's a diary or a messy room, don't invade your child's space unless you have serious cause for concern. This is especially true when it comes to your child's own body. If you must bathe or dress your child at this age, do so with care and with an eye toward preserving your child's privacy and dignity. Cover up private areas during bathing and dressing and use the correct rest room. Ask yourself if what you're doing to or for your child would be OK if the tables were reversed.

- *Pick your battles.* Is a messy room really that big a deal? I'd give anything to have my son back with the motor skills to make a big mess in his room. (OK, take out the moldy pizza.) Put these things into perspective. If it's not a matter of life or death, let it slide—you've got more important dragons to slay.

Key Issues Facing Junior High and High School Students

During this stage, our cute little darlings can turn into increasingly complex beings that we may have trouble recognizing. Have you noticed how children change physically during these years? There is a lot going on with teens inside and out. It's a time of powder-keg emotions and risky behaviors.

Dr. Lisa Boesky (www.drlisab.com) understands the teen years well. She specializes in teen depression, attention-deficit/hyperactivity disorder (ADHD), bipolar disorder, post-traumatic stress disorder, psychosis, conduct disorder, teen suicide and self-injury, and effective behavior management. Boesky works with teens from ages twelve to nineteen, but her work is often relevant up to age twenty-six, because many people with special needs may be functionally, cognitively, and emotionally at ages thirteen to fourteen. Boesky says that the challenges facing middle school students intensify in junior high and high school. Whereas middle schoolers are usually very attached to family, junior high and high schoolers become increasingly more attached to peers—increasing their risk of involvement in behaviors like taking drugs and participating in sexual behaviors. Socialization during the teen years can take on a whole new meaning as kids begin reaching out less to family and more to their peers. This stage can be extra risky for kids with special needs, who may have trouble fitting in along with a strong need to feel accepted. Boesky offers some key strategies for facing this stage of your child's life:

- *Monitor, monitor, monitor!* "Some of these kids may not recognize the consequences of their behaviors, plus it feels good to be accepted by our peers." Boesky suggests that parents monitor their children's friendships, educate them about what real friends are, and discuss high-risk behaviors like smoking and experimenting with alcohol, drugs, and sexuality. Adolescence is a time when parents often begin reaping the rewards of their past efforts. "It's critical that a good parenting foundation is laid early in a child's life, but now it's even more crucial to continue to stay involved in your child's life. During adolescence, parents need to release the reins a bit, but not too much—they still have a profound influence on their child's decision making."

- *Do lots of fun family activities together.* Keep the line of communication open. It's extra important at this age. "Parents need to know what is going on with their children and most kids will open up if they have a good relationship with their parents." Educate them about risky behaviors. "Some of these kids may need to be reminded and re-reminded—and parents are competing against peers." Don't be afraid to ask questions.

- *Keep your child in school.* "We know that one of the biggest risk factors for involvement in risky behaviors is low involvement with school. Any type of participation in academics, sports or favorite clubs, classes and activities is protective."

- *Ask for help.* (Where have you heard that before?) Boesky says as teen issues get more complex, many parents don't know what to do. She suggests that parents utilize school counselors and psychologists if they have any concerns about their children.

- *Be careful about medicating your child.* Medication can help someone who needs it, but Boesky says there's an epidemic of medicating *normal* teen behavior. "A pill should only be provided when absolutely necessary, and it should not be the primary form of treatment." Good parenting is more powerful than any pill! Boesky's words remind us that addressing many challenging teen issues *begins in the home*, with solid parenting decisions made throughout a child's life (as we have stressed throughout this book). Parents *do* make the difference in the lives of their children. *Empowered parents rule.*

JUDY WINTER'S TIPS

The Teen Years

Use the following seven tips to ensure that your child has a good educational experience and a healthy social life, too.

- *Consider adding new support staff.* Many children with special needs have female support staff. If you have a son, this is a good age to consider adding some males to the team, like a tutor, coach, paraprofessional, or Big Brother. Our sons need positive male role models as they age, plus this may help address your child's growing sensitivity to issues like bathroom use and puberty.

- *Encourage friendships.* It's unfortunate, but this is when cliques really do begin to rule the school, making it especially tough for children who have trouble making and keeping friends or those who look or act different. That makes the tip about helping your child cultivate and foster meaningful friendships even more important. Consider involvement in programs like Best Buddies.

- *Let your child take part in extracurricular activities.* By this age, most kids are involved in some kind of after-school activities, which builds a sense of belonging and even promotes physical fitness. It's a great way for your child to explore areas of interest that may help with career planning later. Sports do matter! Much of society and school involves sports. If your child wants to take part, encourage it. Talk with team coaches about how to best include your child on the team, or seek out adapted sports if necessary. The same can be said for participation in music, art, and drama. If your child wants to be part of these activities, help make it happen. It's part of growing up. And don't let your child be treated like the team *mascot*. Set clear goals and expectations.

- *Make good choices about curriculum. Self-determination* is the name of the game. In short, that means that students help guide decisions made about their life and education. They have the freedom to make important life choices. There is an increasing use of this terminology and focus in education. Engage in thoughtful IEP transition planning. Read on to learn more about the importance of transition and curriculum choices. Avoid classroom pullouts! Remember LRE: least restrictive environment under IDEA? Push for support that comes directly into the classroom rather than allow pullout situations, which tend to make children lower their own expectations or feel like they stand out even more. I've often thought that if we pulled everyone out of the classroom who needed help, there would probably be no one left in the classroom except *maybe* the teacher.

- *Talk about sexuality with your child.* I know this is an unnerving discussion for many adults, but it's critical to your child's health, well-being, and safety. Talk about all aspects of sexuality and healthy body image. Depending on your child's level of comprehension and cognitive abilities, discussing good touch–bad touch is an especially important conversation to have to help

(continued on next page)

(continued from previous page)

protect your child from physical and sexual abuse—a serious risk for those with special needs.

- *Choose the most effective way to teach your child about sexuality.* Use age-appropriate books and other materials or seek out the support of professionals in addressing these issues, including issues of sexual activity. Children with special needs (people-first language) should be taught to speak up loudly if they are uncomfortable with something that someone else is trying to do to or with them (think that familiar parenting "stranger" talk). For children with special needs who have speech challenges, it's a good idea to plan how they can best communicate any concerns they may have. Team members should be included in brainstorming such options. As with other children, teaching kids with special needs how to protect themselves is critical. Children must know that it is not only OK but also *necessary* to tell if they are in any way uncomfortable with what is happening to them outside your care.

- *Discuss the driver's license.* It's a right of passage that not every child with special needs will recognize. That said, don't assume your child won't drive. There are many modifications that can be made to vehicles today to grant people with disabilities that much-coveted mobility and independence. Check it out!

 DID YOU KNOW?

If you or your child is in need of immediate mental health intervention—*don't wait!* Contact the National Suicide Hotline: 1-800-SUICIDE (1-800-784-2433) or 1-800-273-TALK (1-800-273-8255), or visit Yellow Ribbon International Suicide Prevention Program/www.YellowRibbon.org / 303-429-3530.

Special Resources for the Teen Years

To help you address this challenging stage a bit more easily, I'm sharing some great adolescent and teen resources right here. There are more on pages 118–121. Please use them!

- *Queen Bees and Wannabes: Helping Your Daughter Survive Cliques, Gossip, Boyfriends, and Other Realities of Adolescence,* by Rosalind Wiseman.

- *Parenting 911: How to Safeguard and Rescue Your 10- to 15-Year-Old from Substance Abuse, Depression, Sexual Encounters, Violence, Failure in School, Danger on the Internet, and Other Risky Situations,* by Charlene C. Giannetti and Margaret Sagarese.

- *What Are You Doing in There? Balancing Your Need to Know with Your Adolescent's Need to Grow,* by Charlene C. Giannetti and Margaret Sagarese.

- *Eight Steps to Help Your Child Survive the Social Jungle,* by Charlene C. Giannetti and Margaret Sagarese.

- *The 7 Habits of Highly Effective Teens: The Ultimate Teenage Success Guide,* by Sean Covey.

- *What's Happening to My Body? Book for Boys: A Growing Up Guide for Parents and Sons,* by Lynda Madaras with Area Madaras.

- *What's Happening to My Body? Book for Girls: A Growing Up Guide for Parents and Daughters,* by Lynda Madaras with Area Madaras.

- *No Body's Perfect: Stories by Teens About Body Image, Self-Acceptance, and the Search for Identity,* by Kimberly Kirberger.

- *Bullies and Victims: Helping Your Children Through the School-yard Battlefield,* by SuEllen Fried and Paula Fried.

- *Friends Who Care,* a diversity awareness program for schools provided by Easter Seals: www.easterseals.org.

- Disabled Sports USA (DS/USA): www.dsusa.org.
- National Sports Center for the Disabled (NSCD): www.nscd.org.
- International Paralympics Committee: www.paralympic.org.

 DID YOU KNOW?

As you and your child face the adolescent years, I highly recommend reading the book *Miracles Happen: One Mother, One Daughter, One Journey,* by Brooke and Jean Ellison. It chronicles the life of a young woman paralyzed from the neck down after being hit by a car the first day of seventh grade. The story details one family's journey of acceptance, recovery, and facing the future—which, for Brooke, now includes a bachelor's and master's degree from Harvard and the pursuit of a Ph.D. It's a reminder that disability can happen to anyone at anytime and demonstrates how to face it head on when it does. A movie based on the book aired in 2004 and was the final project directed by Christopher Reeve. *The Brooke Ellison Story* will help you redefine possibilities, parent involvement, and going to college. Check it out!

 DID YOU KNOW?

Best Buddies is a nonprofit organization whose mission "is to enhance the lives of people with intellectual disabilities (formerly called mental retardation) by providing opportunities for one-on-one friendships and integrated employment." There are programs in fifty states serving middle school, high school, and college-aged students and a Best Buddies Job (employment) and Best Buddies Citizens (for adults). You can find out more about this great organization founded in 1989 by Anthony Shriver at www.bestbuddies.org.

OK, we've addressed lots of critical elements regarding the adolescent and teen years. It's time to add one more element with major impact on your child's overall school success during the middle school to young adult stage: transition.

UNDERSTANDING TRANSITION AND PREPARING FOR THE WORKPLACE AND COLLEGE

Even though the high school graduation rate for students with special needs is improving, it's still pretty dismal. According to a report from the Association for Supervision and Curriculum Development (ASCD) (May 2003, issue 33, *Information Brief*) citing 2001 statistics from the U.S. Department of Education, students with disabilities drop out at twice the rate of all other students (outrageous and depressing, isn't it?), and the rate for minorities with special needs is even more dismal. That makes good transition planning especially crucial to success. As transition coordinator for a Michigan school district and parent of a high school student with cerebral palsy, Chuck Saur lives and breathes transition day in–day out. He knows how important transition planning is, and he models that importance in his decisions as an educator and as an effective advocate for his teenage son, Dan. More about this dad's advocacy in Chapter Six. Saur offers a unique professional-parent perspective on transition.

Transition

First, here are two important definitions that Chuck Saur says you should know:

• *Transition planning.* By at least age sixteen, a student's IEP must include a statement of transition service needs and goals, based on that student's course of study. At this stage, it's important to ask what your child's strengths and interests are. "Good transition planning addresses education goals, including career preparation, life skills, and necessary interagency linkages and services and should start early in a student's life," Saur says. "Think of transition in terms of your own retirement. You aren't going to suddenly walk out of your job and say, 'Now, what am I going to do?' You need time to prepare." Saur says that "transition planning should never be just about placement. We need to constantly look at the student's present level of educational performance and ask where the student *is* relative to where he wants to be."

• *Transition services*. By the time a student is at least age sixteen, transition services must be addressed in the student's IEP. These are services that help the student move successfully from the school setting to adulthood. They include adult services, independent living, job training and employment, attending college, and community involvement. "Once the student is sixteen, parents, schools, and community agencies should start looking at who is likely to provide and/or pay for services for these students when they exit school," Saur says. "Without transition planning, the ball is thrown down the court without knowing if it will be caught. We need to make connections early so students aren't left standing in a fog at the high school door, asking, 'Now, what?'" he explains. "They should walk out saying, 'I know exactly where I'm going and I've got the support I need.'" Saur explains that this is where agency agreements at state and county levels come in. Depending on the needs of the student, the agencies involved in transition services may vary. Students now move from *entitlement* (services mandated by special education rules and IDEA) to *eligibility*. "Everything depends on eligibility, and agency services are not guaranteed. Every agency has different funding streams, service providers, and challenges."

Becoming Independent

Saur explains what parents and students need to know regarding the four key transition areas mandated by IDEA. Start planning early.

- *Independent living.* Ask what the student's aspirations for living independently are. Parents should start early and do everything they can to encourage their children to become as independent as possible. "They need to ask questions about their child's ability to perform daily living skills, like can the student wake up alone, get out of bed, and get dressed alone?"

- *Community connections.* Saur defines community connections as linkages that ensure that children feel a sense of belonging within their community. "The local school district can help with this planning because the district has an array of social and community connections." Parents can involve their children in job sites and teach them about volunteering in the community.

- *Post–secondary learning opportunities.* "Ask what additional learning the student is going to need when he or she exits the school setting," Saur says. "Will the student require occupational training for their career choice? Do they want to attend a community college or a four-year university? What kind of support will the student require to accomplish these goals?"

- *Employment.* Students should work as early as possible on a variety of career explorations. "Finding out where their talents and interests lie is an important part of the IEP team meeting," Saur explains. "The discussion should take place early so thought can be given about how to best help them reach their goals."

For some students, special needs may limit options. Saur says the object for these students is to maximize the level of independence that they can reach. "That means the IEP team must understand what options, obstacles, and community support must be in place before the student exits school.

"Because of my son's physical challenges, I know he might not become a driver for Federal Express," Saur says. "We need to think about options for living, community involvement, and any additional training that will lead him to a career he can enjoy. Dan has expressed a strong interest in meteorology, so we are giving him every opportunity to explore that career choice, by making appearances on our local network news station helping report the weather.

"Here's a child who can't talk and uses a power wheelchair," Saur adds, "and he's doing the weather every morning at his high school and appearing on local television. As a result of this, for the next year Dan's educational team will be aligning everything we can—reading, spelling, math, etc. to a functional level driven by where *Dan* wants to be in the future, and where Dan wants to be is in the broadcast area. As his parents, we're going to do everything we can to help make that happen."

Successful Transition

Saur drives home some key parenting tips for transition success:

- *Start transition planning early in your child's life*. "Focus on getting the educational support your child needs to meet their goals while the student is still in school—for example, the last thing you want to do is have a student do initial career exploration in college." He advises parents to be vigilant in making sure plans made for their children are based on *their* preferences and interests.

- *Involve the student in the decision-making process*. "A critical part of good transition planning is student involvement. The IEP should include a statement describing *the student's* interests, preferences, and post-school goals. This information encourages the student and IEP team members to start thinking early about the student's aspirations for when they exit school—and then plan accordingly."

- *Support your children's dreams*. "An interest in medicine doesn't always mean the child wants to be a neurologist. It may mean he or she wants to go into the medical industry. Parents need to find out *why* their child is attracted to specific careers." Saur believes strongly in supporting the dreams of all students.

This educator dad is pleased with the changes regarding transition in the IDEA 2004 reauthorization (me too). Like early intervention, the focus is now strength based, based on the interests of the child and focused on attainable postsecondary goals. "Professionals must now identify postsecondary goals in the IEP—and we will be held accountable for them." The law is also clear now about including academics in transition goals. Saur sums up four key changes to transition under IDEA:

- "We are focusing away from what we write (paperwork) to *what we do* (action)."
- "We are moving away from compliance to *quality*."
- "We are moving away from what we promised to do, to what we actually *provide*."
- "We are moving from promises to *outcomes*. And that's cool!" he says. It's also great news for your child.

Preparing for College

According to the 1994 U.S. Census, one in four college students has special needs, a number bound to increase in the future with better education. And these students are keeping pace with their peers' graduation rates. You're not alone in pursuing this exciting dream. It *is* possible.

It's important for you to understand that when children transition out of high school, they are no longer supported by IDEA and an IEP. Now your friends are the Americans with Disabilities Act of 1990 (ADA) and Section 504. According to the U.S. Department of Justice ADA home page, the Americans with Disabilities Act (ADA) prohibits discrimination on the basis of disability in employment, state and local government, public accommodations, commercial facilities, transportation, and telecommunications. To learn more about this federal law and how it affects those with special needs, visit www.ada.gov.

Children are now facing challenges they may never have faced before. Education is no longer a *right* guaranteed by IDEA, but an *opportunity* for which your child must apply. The IEP is now history; everything is student driven. Most colleges today offer disability support offices and services to assist and support students with special needs, support that may be crucial to success. If the school you're considering doesn't have such support, reconsider.

If you and your child have made good use of transition planning and services before your child exits high school, you'll have an idea of where your child is headed and who or what will support her in reaching her postsecondary school dreams. Here are a couple of resources to get you started on your quest. There are more listed under Special Resources on pages 118–121.

- ThinkCollege.net. You'll find great information, links, and lots of student voices.

- Students with Disabilities: Preparing for Postsecondary Education: Know Your Rights and Responsibilities: U.S. Department of Education pamphlet: http://www.ed.gov/ocr/transition.html.

 ## JOHNNIE TUITEL'S TIPS

Surviving the College Years

Johnnie Tuitel offers three key strategies that will help your child succeed during the college years.

- *Seek out necessary support services.* "Have the guts to ask for help, even if that means with tying your shoes. Then your disability becomes part of the human condition and a powerful gift."

- *Find out what you are good at—and stand up for yourself.* "If you can't speak, find someone who can speak up for you!" (and access necessary state-of-the-art technology).

- *Take Johnnie Tuitel's advice to parents.* It's short and to the point: "Let go!"

Preparing for the Workplace: One Educator's Voice

For students with special needs who do not plan on getting their high school diploma (consider this carefully!) or attending college, preparing for the workplace is especially critical to their future independence.

Preparing students with special needs for a successful transition from the classroom to the workplace is what Michigan special educator Sue Rundborg does best. We first met Rundborg as Carrie Clise's teacher in Chapter Three. Rundborg has spent more than a decade building a strong classroom program focused on job readiness. Her students work at job sites as volunteers, hoping to be hired upon graduation—80 percent of her students are placed in volunteer work settings like Burger King, Pizza Hut, and Wal-Mart.

The program includes a van for transportation and a job coach, who goes to job sites with the students. "We are a full-blown program," Rundborg says. With her job coach, Rundborg keeps close tabs on all job sites to ensure smooth sailing. Daily work commitments are for two-hour blocks of time, and Friday mornings are reserved for delivering food to the homebound. "It's important to give back to communities in which we live and work," she says.

Rundborg's program provides a job training coach and work experiences. Another special education teacher in a school district nearby provides students with the important educational and social component of attending a regular high school. Both teachers work closely with important community agencies. Their goal is to place as many students as possible into job training.

Here is Rundborg's advice on preparing students for the workplace:

- *Take a new look at academics.* If a student isn't college bound, make classroom work functional, and focus on job skills that help increase workplace success.

- *Provide students with a variety of experiences in their own community.* This is where acceptance is more likely and transportation is less of an issue. Such efforts can result in the perfect job with the perfect employer.

- *Don't get isolated in your classroom.* Network with other professionals and involve local community agencies.

- *Begin with a job coach.* This will ensure a smooth transition and ease the minds of business owners who may be reluctant to commit to the program.

- *Plan for the exit IEP.* (This is the final IEP before graduation.) Invite anyone who is key to the child's successful transition to the workplace to participate. These include representatives from key community agencies, the student, parents, and employers. Rundborg provides a list of the past job sites, the names of supervisors, and skills required for the job, information that helps prevent inappropriate work placements.

- *Exhaust opportunities to teach skills in a natural setting.* For example, take working students out to lunch instead of brown-bagging it, to enhance money skills, ordering skills, and eating skills.

Special Resources

Here are a few resources that can be helpful for addressing transition and for preparing your child for the workplace.

Technology

- *Ability Magazine*: www.abilitymagazine.com: offers great links to valuable resources addressing independent living, health, education, employment, assistive technology, and the like, for a wide range of special needs and the link to Apple Computer technology: www.apple.com/ability.

- *Assistive Technology Act of 2004*: summary of the law that improves access to technology for those with special needs,

Committee on Education and the Workforce: http://edworkforce.house.gov.

- Bridge School: www.bridgeschool.org: for students with severe speech challenges. Offers training and programs in alternative forms of communication and summer camp opportunities, including for siblings.

- *Computer Resources for People with Disabilities: A Guide to Assistive Technologies, Tools, and Resources for People of All Ages,* by Alliance for Technology and Stephen Hawking.

- The Alliance for Technology Access (ATA): http://www.ataccess.org.

- U.S. Department of Education (USDE): www.ed.gov: *College Students with Disabilities and Assistive Technology: A Desk Reference Guide.*

Transition

- The National Center on Secondary Education (NCSET): www.ncset.org.

- National Information Center for Children and Youth with Disabilities (NICHCY): www.nichcy.org: postsecondary transition.

- Best Buddies International: www.bestbuddies.org.

- Chuck Saur, transition coordinator, Kent ISD: ChuckSaur@KentISD.org.

High School, College and the Workplace

- *Your Child: Sexuality and Kids with Disabilities or Chronic Illness: A Resource List:* University of Michigan Health Systems: www.med.umich.edu/1libr/yourchild/disabsex/htm.

- *Sexuality Education for Children and Youth with Disabilities* (thirty-seven-page news digest) NICHCY (National Clearing

House for Children and Youth with Disabilities):
www.nichcy.org.

- National Traffic Safety Administration (NTSA):
  http://www.ntsa.gov: offers the guide *Adapting Motor Vehicles for People with Disabilities*.

- CollegeBoard.com: information on entrance exams and accommodations.

- Job Accommodation Network (JAN): janweb.icdi.wvu.edu.

- *Job Search Handbook for People with Disabilities*, by Daniel J. Ryan.

- *Keys to Workplace Skills and Support for People with Disabilities*, by Michael J. Callanhan and J. Bradley Garner.

- *Moving Violations: War Zones, Wheelchairs, and Declarations of Independence*, by John Hockenberry.

Miscellaneous

- The National Arts and Disabilities Center (NADC):
  http:nadc.ucla.edu.

- Dancing Wheels: a professional dance troupe for dancers of all abilities, including wheelchair users: www.gggreg.com/dancingwheels.htm.

- Camps for kids with special needs: www.kidscamps.com.

- Abilitations free catalogue: www.abilitations.com/equipment/play.

- Permobil: www.permobil.com: considered world innovators in power wheelchair design.

- National PTA: www.pta.org: search for bullying resources.

- *Edutopia: The New World of Learning* (The George Lucas Foundation): www.edutopia.org.

- Many states may now offer their own Web sites, but I think the Center for Educational Networking (CEN) (Michigan

Department of Education) is one of the best, with breaking news, links, access to sister sites nationwide, and publications like *Leading Change* (which includes *my* work): www.cenmi.org.

- American Dental Association: www.ada.org: oral health and special needs.
- Paws with a Cause (PAWS): www.pawswithacause.org: assistance dogs.
- *Living with Spina Bifida: A Guide for Families and Professionals*, by Adrian Sandler.
- *When Someone You Love Has a Mental Illness*, by Rebecca Woolis.

Whew! We've just survived a couple of rather intense chapters together, including some of that unnerving legal stuff.

Congratulations! You have survived the first half of *Breakthrough Parenting for Children with Special Needs*. We've covered lots of important ground together. And I hope you're feeling increasingly empowered in your new parenting role. Let's turn our attention now to Chapter Six and celebrate personal advocacy, effective communication (yours), and working well with professionals.

6

ADVOCATING FOR TECHNIQUES AND PROGRAMS THAT WORK

No one can make you feel inferior without your consent.
—Eleanor Roosevelt

You have probably noticed by now that throughout *Breakthrough Parenting for Children with Special Needs,* good parenting choices and solid advocacy resulting in parent empowerment have been touted as the most powerful factors in helping kids with special needs lead better lives. That's because they are!

The information presented in this chapter will help you build on the advocacy skills that you still need in order to reach your important parenting goals, by addressing effective communication and working well with professionals.

I'll also introduce you to music therapy and conductive education, two great programs that work for many children and adults with special needs. And we'll revisit the law (only briefly!) to define *mediation* and *due process*—actions you can take when, despite all your hard work and positive thinking, you meet a major educational brick wall that stops you dead in your parenting tracks.

Finally, I've thrown in some special tips for the professionals we work with, so they can have a better understanding and respect for the valuable parenting voice. That heart-to-heart discussion is long overdue.

We begin with the story of one amazing mom of an adult child with Down syndrome, who, through her tireless advocacy in the entertainment industry, has helped many children and adults with special needs reach for the stars, including her own son. And she's not finished yet!

A SUCCESS STORY

Parents of children with special needs are used to hearing all those limiting words about what their kids will never achieve, so it's no wonder their career goals for their children were once limited to bagging groceries or stocking supermarket shelves, although these are important jobs, too.

Kids with special needs also dream of becoming artists, musicians, or dancers—even Hollywood stars. That makes it vital that parents and professionals foster the creative gifts of children with special needs, much as they do with other talented children *and* from an early age.

That's exactly what Gail Williamson has done for the past twenty-five years for her son Blair, an actor with Down syndrome, and for many others with special needs. Williamson is executive director of the Down Syndrome Association of Los Angeles (DSALA) and former coordinator of the Talent Development and Industry Relations Division of the Media Access Office (MAO) in Hollywood, California.

Until budget cuts cost her the contract position with the MAO in 2003, Williamson spent twelve years serving as the first disabilities coordinator and acting coach for such successful television programs as *ER*, *Touched by an Angel*, *Family Law*, *Law & Order: SUV* and *The Guardian*.

Her role included developing new talent and helping experienced actors with special needs set goals—a commitment she now continues in her role for the DSALA, responsibilities that include growing its new casting division.

Williamson's work in the entertainment industry first took creative root in 1980, with the premature birth of her son. When two school psychologists later asked if she was considering acting lessons for Blair, Williamson was surprised. "I just thought Blair was just a little show-off," Williamson says. "I had no idea what I should do about all the comments about Blair's acting potential," she explains, "but I felt I should pursue them."

At age ten, Blair was asked by Special Olympics to audition for a thirty-second national commercial for Procter & Gamble. He walked away with the part. And his mother discovered an exciting new career in entertainment!

Williamson's son now attends a day program in Los Angeles, where he is a power lifter for Special Olympics and part of a well-known L.A. bell and chime choir that performs yearly at the Dorothy Chandler Pavilion. His acting credits now include theater, commercials, film, and television, including *ER*, *Nip/Tuck*, and the hit CBS series *CSI*.

"He got murdered on *CSI!*" Williamson says. "It's every actor's dream to be a corpse on CSI because they get to do a lot of acting in flashbacks!"

In addition to commercials for Proctor & Gamble and Macy's, Blair's work now includes several independent movies, including *My Antonia* (USA Network), and he just booked the feature film *Unknown*, starring James Caviezel (who played Jesus in *The Passion of the Christ*). *Unknown* is a drama-thriller scheduled for release in 2006. That's exciting stuff!

Williamson, whose phone calls are now taken by many of Hollywood's top industry players, hasn't lost her fire for making the dreams of actors with special needs come true. Only the organization's name has changed. "I'm riding the wave of disability awareness that now exists in Hollywood," she says with pride, "and I'm going to ride it well until the next big wave comes along."

In her new role as an advocate for the DSALA, Gail Williamson reminds us that good advocates hold the power to effect remarkable change in a child's life and in the lives of others. Let's see how you can create some advocacy magic of your own. Get inspired. Then get busy.

Embracing Advocacy

One of the greatest challenges facing parents of children with special needs is learning how to advocate effectively for their children. Any effort that directly helps individuals with special needs (and their siblings) improve the quality of their life today is *my* definition of advocacy.

First, ask yourself if the choices you are currently making—whether during an IEP meeting, at the doctor's office, during a public outing, or at the dinner table—will help your child have a better life. Will your actions also have positive impact on other children—and help lead to important societal change?

Responsible advocacy comes with the special needs territory. It's so important that I'm including a second example of parenting advocacy excellence to inspire you further—and to make up for having no success story in Chapter Five.

The Power of Parenting Advocacy

Chuck and Sue Saur give new meaning to parental involvement in education—and help redefine the power of advocacy. With an unwavering commitment to their now seventeen-year-old son, Dan, who has cerebral palsy, the Grand Rapids, Michigan, couple helped make conductive education a reality for children nationwide with motor impairments.

We first met Chuck Saur while exploring *transition* in Chapter Five.

Conductive education (CE) is a comprehensive, Hungarian-based program for children with motor disorders like cerebral palsy and spina bifida. You can learn more about CE under Programs That Work on page 129.

In 1995, the family's participation in a CE camp in Ontario, Canada, dramatically altered the direction of their lives. They returned from the camp with a renewed vision of increased physical independence for Dan, a wheelchair user.

The Saurs' parenting vision fueled a grassroots effort to bring CE from Eastern Europe to West Michigan and earned the support of Aquinas College, a private, liberal arts college in Grand Rapids, Michigan. Today the Conductive Learning Center (CLC) (www.aquinas.edu/clc) is a successful year-round program and training school for conductive education.

But before the dream became reality, these parents did tons of groundwork. Once they had experienced CE at camp and discovered the program in Hungary, they took a second mortgage on their house to finance an intensive six-month program for Dan in Budapest, the home of conductive education.

Sue Saur traveled to this large Eastern European city with her two sons. She couldn't speak the language and had to carry her fifty-five pound son up and down the stairs when the elevator didn't work.

With Dan immersed in CE in Budapest, Chuck Saur knocked on several doors at home in West Michigan before garnering support from Aquinas College for a pilot program, then joined forces with other parents of motor-impaired children to create the first parent-driven summer program for CE in Michigan. It was the beginning of realizing bigger family dreams.

Chuck Saur recalls the exact moment when Dan first cast his own fishing rod into a lake, a task that Chuck had always performed for his son. Today Dan can write his own name and take steps with support. He can sit up in bed and rub the sleep from his eyes with once rigid hands and recite his own bedtime prayer.

"It's hard to explain the magnitude of what conductive education has meant to our family," Chuck Saur explained. "We've gone from thinking about what we can do for Dan to celebrating what he can do for himself, and that difference is huge."

So are the results of their determined efforts to advocate for this program, and for their son. Here are a few of the Saurs' suggestions for successfully implementing a new educational program and for becoming a more effective parenting advocate.

- *Commit yourself.* The Saur family committed years of their time, energy, and personal resources to bring conductive education to West Michigan—a passionate mission that continues today.

- *Educate yourself.* Conductive education began in Hungary in 1945, and it's recognized in many parts of the world, including Canada, England, and New Zealand. But it's relatively new to the United States and is generating much discussion. Parents *must understand* the programs they are trying to promote. If you don't get it, chances are good others won't either. Chuck Saur educated himself and studied the Hungarian program before seeking critical educational backing. He *knew* what he was selling—and he *believed* strongly in the product.

- *Don't give up.* The Saur family refused to be discouraged by the resistance they faced working toward a big goal, and they never gave up on their parenting dreams—or on their son.

- *Never underestimate parent power.* Don't underestimate your power to effect amazing change. The Saurs' commitment to ensuring greater independence for Dan fueled them during tough days. Chuck Saur stresses that the first three CE summer programs were supported and fueled mainly by *parents* of children in the program, who did everything from helping the conductors solve immigration problems and get settled in this country to providing snacks for the children. That's parent power at work!

Recognizing the Power of Advocacy

We've learned from Gail Williamson and the Saur family that a parent's advocacy can be a powerful impetus for important societal change. But you don't have to go to Hollywood or go to Budapest to bring about positive change. Even small actions can result in big payoffs for a child.

For some parents, advocacy may mean joining a parent advisory committee (PAC) or a national disability organization. Some parents will start their own groups, whereas others may dislike the political agendas that can be associated with organized groups.

My suggestion regarding participation in such groups is to *choose group memberships carefully.* The advocacy road that one chooses to take isn't nearly as important as why one chooses to take it. If being part of an organized parenting or other group speaks to you, seek them out. But ask some tough questions first:

- Who does the group serve and why? What is their approach?
- How can this group help me to better serve my child?
- How does the group work to resolve conflict?
- How has this group served parents and children successfully?
- Does this group serve the best interests of parents and children?

I believe in empowering each parent to become the best advocate that he or she can be, independent of group membership, by utilizing all of the strategies that you have learned in this book so far and those still to come. No one group can possibly resolve all the challenges that come with parenting a child with special needs. Families expecting more may be sorely disappointed.

JUDY WINTER'S TIPS
Advocacy

You can advocate in a big way or in a quiet way. Each counts profoundly—you choose what works for you!

- *Celebrate the power of one.* Your own actions may be as grand as accepting an invitation to serve on a statewide commission on disability concerns or as quietly powerful as helping your child learn to read, use technology, or prepare well for an IEP meeting. Your advocacy may include writing letters regarding funding, improving accessibility, or helping those with special needs find affordable housing.

- *Don't bite off more than you can chew.* Most parents of children with special needs can remember days when the most they could do for their child was to get out of bed and put one foot in front of the other. On these challenging days, perhaps that is advocacy enough. You can scale bigger peaks another day.

DID YOU KNOW?

According to the March of Dimes (www.marchofdimes.com), one in eight babies in the United States is born too soon. Some of these babies will face lifelong disabilities. The mission of the March of Dimes is "to improve the health of babies by preventing birth defects and infant mortality." Check it out!

PROGRAMS THAT WORK

Along this unpredictable parenting journey, you will probably run into some well-meaning folks bearing great ideas they just know will benefit your child. Say thanks—politely—but don't be pressured into making decisions about programs you aren't comfortable with, especially when they come from people who haven't a clue as to what it takes to parent a child with special needs.

That said, here are two programs that changed my son's life. Maybe they'll work for your child. *You* decide, and then check out some ideas of your own!

Music Therapy

For seven years, Eric thrived in the Music Therapy Program at Michigan State University (MSU), which, when established in 1944, was the first program of its kind in the world. Eric was identified as having strong musical interests at age three by an MSU professor of early childhood music, who described him as *a child full of music*. She suggested that we enroll Eric in music classes—and we wisely followed her professional advice. It paid off in spades.

Cindy Lu Edgerton, MM, MT-BC, is a board-certified music therapist with a master's of music from MSU. She worked with Eric for most of his life.

According to Edgerton, music therapists work on nonmusical goals and objectives and through music address the individualized physical, cognitive, emotional, and social needs of children and adults with special needs. Edgerton explains that research indicates that music stimulates and engages many parts of the brain, making it an especially effective (and fun) tool in addressing a wide range of special needs. Music therapy is considered appropriate for a variety of special needs, including cerebral palsy, autism, Down syndrome, traumatic brain injury (TBI), Alzheimer's, and others.

Music therapy affects Edgerton's clients in the following ways:

- *Singing* encourages verbal communication, socialization skills, cognition, and self-expression.

- *Playing the kazoo* helps elicit and develop speech. "I've worked with many nonverbal children who first began vocalizing by playing the kazoo," Edgerton says.

- *Playing a musical instrument* builds gross and fine motor skills, enhances verbal communication, and helps clients better understand cause and effect. Edgerton says that playing the guitar, drums, and other instruments can provide clients with an immediate and successful form of self-expression, something that may be elusive for those with special needs.

Eric's involvement in music therapy resulted in some remarkable gains, including enhanced motor skills, greater communication skills, heightened self-esteem, and increased motivation in his daily activities, including homework. Before he died, my son was composing and wanting to study music at MSU—a dream we planned to fully support.

Today the Eric 'RicStar' Winter Music Therapy Summer Camp at Michigan State University offers individuals of all ages and abilities the opportunity to experience the power of music firsthand. The yearly camp continues our son's remarkable musical legacy.

Conductive Education

As we've discussed, conductive education (CE) is an exciting, comprehensive program for children with motor disorders. The program is now catching fire in the United States. After a segment about CE aired on 60 *Minutes II* in 2004, demand for access to the program in the United States has increased dramatically.

Andrea Benyovszky is program director of the Conductive Learning Center in Grand Rapids, Michigan, which serves children and adolescents with cerebral palsy, spina bifida, and other motor challenges. "Conductive education involves the complex development of the *whole personality* instead of just focusing on motor and functional development," Benyovszky explains. "It's a form of *active learning* because it transfers educational principles into rehabilitation."

In short, extensively trained practitioners, who are called conductors, work very hard to maximize a child's physical, cognitive, and social development. The program addresses everything from self-care; to play; to cognitive, social, and intellectual development; to parent education. Kids are encouraged to do things for themselves, which leads to increased self-confidence and greater motor independence.

CE was developed by Dr. Andras Peto in 1945 in Budapest, Hungary. Benyovszky says that CE is fueled by the theory that the central nervous system has the capacity to form new neural connections, even when there's previous neurological damage. By repeating specific tasks, integrating intentional movement, and adding education components, Benyovszky states the desired developmental gains may be realized.

The program focuses on meeting individual goals in a group setting of peers who exhibit various levels of special needs involvement.

Eric took part in the CLC program from age seven until passing away at age twelve. His impressive gains included minutes of independent sitting (huge for him), significantly reduced tone and increased head control, the ability to eat solids, increased speech (including "I love you"), greater self-confidence, and the ability to hug back (priceless).

Along with music therapy and enrollment in a regular preschool and inclusive education, conductive education was the most important program that Eric was involved in.

Caution! Programs may vary in quality. When considering any program, it is important not only to think outside the parenting box but also to thoroughly research any program before enrolling your child. The CLC is one of more than thirty such programs in the United States, but in 2004, it was the *only* program directly associated with and supervised by the International Peto Institute for Conductive Education in Budapest, Hungary.

Don't make important program decisions for your child based solely on emotion. What works for one child may not work for your child. Do your homework. And be sure to check out all the Special Resources on page 143.

COMMUNICATING EFFECTIVELY

Most parents and professionals agree that good communication is a critical part of the parent-professional partnership, especially in regard to educating students with special needs. Most would probably also agree that when adults strive for good communication, our kids win.

So how is it that too often our words and actions don't match? If there's one thing I've learned after parenting both a teenager and a child with cerebral palsy, it's this: in nearly every situation that requires positive resolution, effective communication begins with *me*—not the other guy. You heard me right! Novel concept, huh?

Educators argue that communication breakdowns often result from the demands of unreasonable and unrealistic parents. Parents counter this argument with their own convincing tales of professional arrogance and the stubborn refusal to recognize parents' valuable input regarding their children. Fact is, there's plenty of arrogance and resistance alive and well on both sides of these arguments—something we *must* change.

All those emotional and angry accusations that we sometimes fling at each other is exactly what gets in the way of good communication and productive working relationships. I call it the *invisible fence syndrome:* parents and professionals perched on opposing sides of the educational fence, staring each other down, each side refusing to allow the other to step foot on their sacred turf.

Too few are willing to risk venturing across this emotional line because of egos, credentials, turf, budgets, intimidation, parenting rights, and legal implications. We each own responsibility for communication breakdowns. And each of us is responsible for removing a piece of the ugly invisible fence that separates us, picket by picket. That fence is costing our children dearly.

Ultimately, it doesn't matter what is going on around you or who's doing what to whom or who's got which shiny new professional title. Get past that stuff. What matters most is what *you* are doing to improve the situation through your own actions. We can't control or change the behaviors of others. But we sure as heck can determine our own. That's the beauty of free will and making good choices. Most of us could benefit from upping our communication game. Our kids are counting on us, and we cannot afford to let them down. We can help change their lives by joining together and by communicating well with each other.

A Personal Story: The Power of Communication

My son's vocabulary consisted of approximately fifteen words. He made me think about my communication efforts every single day of his life. As Eric struggled, with spunk and determination, to speak simple words, he reminded me of their true value and compelled me to really listen to him.

Some of us talk way too much, yet say very little. We use emotionally charged words to judge the actions of others, when we'd be better off using them to judge our own. Such poor communication efforts reveal a disturbing misuse of the remarkable gift of language.

Communication is a privilege and a blessing. That's something else my preteen taught me as he struggled with every ounce of his being to say the three simple words—*I love you*. You bet I heard them!

Eric taught me to talk less and listen more and reminded me to make sure I had really heard what was said before reacting. He taught me to slow down in my efforts to communicate with him, especially when I was rushed for time or under pressure by *others* to prove what *he* knew.

Eric taught me to treat people with respect, instead of approaching individuals armed to do battle, even when I had just cause. After seeing my son's efforts at simple communication, I'm embarrassed to admit that adults who usually speak clearly and effortlessly (and are pretty well educated) often fail miserably in our efforts to communicate well. It's inexcusable.

When it comes to effective communication, my son, with his limited speech and mobility, wise eyes, enchanting smile, bright mind, and refreshing lack of arrogance, and with no college degree, was my greatest life teacher—and the *real expert*.

The best way to bring about positive change in others is to model it yourself. Here are some suggestions to help you do just that:

- *Treat others the way you would like to be treated*. It's a great rule in most situations. Try it and see what happens.
- *Be sensitive to other people's needs and desires*. It's the other side of the sensitivity coin. Others are not just like you, so pay close attention to what *they* may be feeling, too. They also have needs.
- *Choose to react positively, no matter how someone else communicates with you*. Responding with anger, intimidation, and

threats can make it more difficult to get your child the services he or she needs today. Find positive, less stressful ways to get your point across.

- *Repeat back what you think you heard the person say.* Do this to ensure that you really heard it right, *before* you react, especially if the discussion is heated.

- *Pay attention to body language.* You can learn a lot by observing people's posture, eye contact, and facial expressions. Do they seem nervous, arrogant, bored, friendly? Are they paying attention to what's being said, nodding in agreement (or foaming at the mouth!)? Watch your own body language. Use good eye contact, sit up tall, offer a firm handshake (no "dishrags"), and stop fidgeting: actions that may influence how others view you and treat you. They are checking you out, too.

- *Set a good example.* Model appropriate behavior even when it's tough. Remember, by responding confidently and with class, you may just become a catalyst for much-needed change. Be a stellar example—that's how we *can* change others.

- *Seek professional support.* If communication still breaks down, pursue mediation or legal support. It's OK to do this. But try to work things out first. And don't threaten litigation every time something doesn't go your way. Work it out!

Here are a couple of easy communication tips to remember: (a) talk less, listen more (and please *don't* use profanity) and (b) be *proactive* in your communication (not reactive).

JUDY WINTER'S TIPS
Working with Professionals

These tips will stand you in good stead when you work with professionals—and they aren't that tough!

- *Be respectful and communicate well.*

(continued on next page)

(continued from previous page)

- *Be prepared for all meetings.*

- *Be on time.* Respect time constraints and commitments of others.

- *Listen to professional concerns and work together to resolve them.*

- *Remember to say please and thank you whenever appropriate.* Sometimes the simplest actions are the most effective of all!

- *Agree on a regular means of communication.* This could be e-mail, a notebook to write in and then send back and forth daily, a phone call, or scheduled meetings.

- *Respond to and address discipline, homework, and absenteeism issues promptly.* Don't waste anyone's time or energy making excuses for your poor behavior or less-than-stellar parenting choices.

Strategies for Professionals Working with Families with Special Needs

LaVelle Gipson-Tansil (gipson@msu.edu) is a faculty specialist in the MSU Department of Family and Child Ecology and an educator-teacher-trainer for early childhood educators.

For two years, this outstanding educator helped me create a firm foundation for Eric's learning—and helped solidify my belief in his right to a good education. She reminds us that children often succeed or fail based on the efforts of the responsible adults in their lives.

Here are a few of her suggestions for professionals hoping to interact more successfully with families of children with special needs:

- *Understand and support families in the context of who they are.*

Learn about family traditions, customs, and ethnicity. Home visits, parent surveys, and questionnaires are tools that can help you obtain such information. Gipson-Tansil suggests asking parents what they want and need. Don't assume you know the answers—and share good resources willingly. "Be careful not to form opinions without good information."

- *Recognize both a family's gifts and limitations, then work within those constraints*. "Our professional goal is to help families create the kind of nurturing environment that supports literacy for *all* children. Avoid judging families!"

- *Take advantage of professional development*. Stay current on timely topics and vary your teaching approach. Try to focus on individual learning styles that can help you reach diverse families. Gipson-Tansil says everyone learns differently. "Some people learn best by talking, while others learn best by writing information down."

- *Create an environment that provides all children with opportunities for expression*. Prepare a classroom with a variety of learning opportunities for individual and small and large group settings whenever appropriate to allow *all* children to participate.

Thanks to outstanding educators like Gipson-Tansil, I love teachers! I think that next to parenting, it's the most noble, important job there is. We are both responsible for the future of a child. We both work incredibly hard, often without enough resources, finances, and training. And we both often get judged harshly by others about how we do or don't measure up.

I've met educators who restored my faith in education—and parents who should be deemed saints. We have lots more in common than it may first appear.

That said, I've also met parents who probably shouldn't have kids and teachers who probably shouldn't be in the classroom. And I'm pretty darn convinced that most of us can do better by our kids—by putting aside egos and working well together.

JUDY WINTER'S TIPS

Professionals

Here are some tips that will go a long way in helping professionals interact more productively with families of kids with special needs:

- *Recognize the importance of open, honest, and respectful communication among professionals and families.* And model it accordingly. Remember that you are talking about someone's *child.* Someone's flesh and blood! Would what you are saying and doing be good enough for your own child? Be sensitive about what you say and how you present it.

- *Never forget that children with special needs are people first.* Try not to define these children or their families by a disability.

- *Include parents in important decisions regarding their child wherever possible.* Teamwork is vital to the success of children with special needs, and families *do* have great information to share. Access it.

- *Work hard to promote and model dynamic partnerships between professionals and families.* Share successful ideas with your peers.

- *Highlight the strengths of a child or family before addressing the challenges at hand.* Focus on the needs of the child.

- *Never underestimate the potential of any child, including those with special needs.* Let's all try to raise the bar of expectations, shall we?

- *Avoid using limiting labels and outdated terms when discussing children.* Words are mighty powerful. So—please watch your language.

- *Adhere to the laws protecting the rights of individuals with special needs.* Refrain from indulging in "water-cooler" and "teacher's-lounge" gossip. That's neither positive nor productive. Don't say nasty stuff about kids and families (think slander), and challenge your peers to join you in upholding the highest standards of this noble profession.

- *Check for personal biases regarding individuals with special needs and work hard to change them.* Seek management support and professional training if you find yourself struggling. Don't pretend you don't have biases—most of us *do*. Acknowledging them is the first step toward change. Ask for the support you need.

- *Model leadership designed to help all children and families become more successful, no matter how small the gain.* Ask yourself what *you* have to learn from a particularly challenging situation. In the end, that's what it's all about anyway—for all of us. Please don't call parents Mom or Dad. They aren't your parents. Use their names. It's more respectful and more appropriate.

- *Advocate for needed change within your own profession.* Don't make the mistake of thinking your profession is immune from making less-than-noble decisions—it's not. We are all human and we all make mistakes, no matter what our roles. We can all make better choices.

- *Never forget that one person can make a difference in the life of a child.* That someone could be you. What an incredible honor! Do it justice.

Please also see the Bill of Rights for Professionals on page 222.

UNDERSTANDING MEDIATION AND DUE PROCESS

If you find yourself in the middle of a pretty good disagreement with your child's school (it happens), and your educational concerns don't seem to be getting resolved (that happens, too), here's a *brief* explanation about your recourse for dispute resolution (mediation and due process).

For more detailed information, visit my favorite sources for this piece:

- www.Wrightslaw.org. By now, this may be your new best friend!
- The Center for Educational Networking (CEN), Michigan Department of Education (MDE): www.cenmi.org. This site has great links.
- www.google.com. Do a Google search. You'll get more than you need.

Now let's take a closer look at these two techniques for conflict resolution: mediation and due process.

Mediation

Here's what you need to know about mediation:

- It's an informal, face-to-face meeting, where parents and school personnel work to resolve differences (disputes) with the help of a neutral third party.
- The goal is to resolve disagreements in a friendlier meeting— before filing formal complaints and pursuing due process. (Please give mediation all you've got!)
- Mediators don't decide who's right or who's full of it. (They don't take sides, including yours. Sorry.) Their job is to foster the kind of communication that helps resolve differences and replace "opposing sides" with teamwork and good solutions.
- Mediation services are free of charge to families, as mandated under IDEA. That's good news!
- Mediation is voluntary. *You* decide if you want to do this.
- The dispute is resolved by the parties involved, not by the mediator. There's parenting power here!

If you have a dispute to resolve, *this* is the way to go. This may also be a good time to revisit Communicating Effectively on page 132.

Unfortunately, mediation doesn't always work. So then you file a formal *complaint* with your state department of education. The result will be a *due process* hearing. You really don't want to go there . . .

Due Process

Here's what you need to know about due process:

- It's scheduled once a formal complaint has been filed. It's going to get more stressful now. Expect it to be more adversarial, with lawyers and expert witnesses involved. Oh, no!

- It takes more time. Your stress is increasing by the minute.

- It's *resolved and decided by a third party*. You've got a 50/50 chance.

- The decision may be appealed to state or federal courts. Unfortunately, that means more unnerving legal and expert lingo.

Try to avoid due process if at all possible. Instead, practice being an IEP (increasingly empowered parent, remember?) and use all the tools you have learned in this book and elsewhere to avoid escalating to a point of no return in the first place. You won't regret it.

Man, just talking about educational legal disputes makes my stomach queasy. Let's move on to more pleasant stuff, shall we?

SPECIAL TIPS

These tips will help guide you to become a more effective child advocate by developing better communication skills and encouraging you to work with professionals as a dynamic team.

- *Keep good school records.* As with your child's medical records, it's important to keep good records regarding your child's education, including IEP paperwork, copies of assessments and other professional documents, communication notes, report cards, and homework samples. Use colorful notebooks, folders, and labels to make this less institutional, and update information regularly.

- *Indulge yourself.* After an especially rough meeting, take time to treat yourself: go to the park or the zoo, rent a funny movie, order pizza, or get a massage. These encounters can take a toll on you physically, emotionally, and spiritually. You need to refuel. No matter how prepared you were, adrenaline was still pumping.

- *Get help with your literacy issues.* A 1992 U.S. Department of Education (USDE) survey reports that 23 percent, or forty-four million, Americans are functionally illiterate—making it tough for some parents to help their children with homework.

A lot of people are embarrassed about asking for help to address literacy difficulties. Don't be. You're a hero for helping yourself and your child succeed. If you're struggling with adult literacy issues, get help. Contact the following organizations—and watch your own world expand!

- The National Institute for Literacy (NIFL): www.nifl.gov/nifl/faqs.html.
- The National Institute for Literacy Hotline: 1-800-228-8813.
- The National Center for Family Literacy (NCFL): www.famlit.org.
- The Family Literacy InfoLine: 1-877-FAMLIT (1-877-326-5481).

Special Resources

You have read about some great resources in the pages of this chapter. Now, here are a number of related resources that can provide you with more helpful information on the key subjects highlighted in Chapter Six.

Entertainment Industry/Down Syndrome

- Gail Williamson: gail@dsala.org.
- Down Syndrome Association of Los Angeles (DSALA): www.dsala.org.
- Actors' Equity Association (AEA): www.actorsequity.org.
- American Federation of Radio and Television Artists (AFTRA): www.aftra.org.
- Screen Actors Guild (SAG): www.scag.org.
- The Non-Traditional Casting Project (NTCP): www.ntcp.org.

Music Therapy

- American Music Therapy Association: www.musictherapy.org.
- For worldwide links: www.musictherapyworld.net.
- Eric 'RicStar' Winter Music Therapy Summer Camp/ Community Music School, Michigan State University (MSU): www.msu.edu/~commusic.

Conductive Education

- Inter-American Conductive Education Association (IACEA): www.iacea.org.
- The Conductive Learning Center (CLC), Grand Rapids, Michigan: www.aquinas.edu/clc.

Dispute Resolution

- *Getting to Yes: Negotiating Agreement Without Giving In*, by Roger Fisher and William Ury.

Special Note

Coverage of special needs by the mainstream media has increased dramatically since 2000. Let them know you approve. Gail Williamson suggests going online to appropriate Web sites and writing an e-mail, or a fax, or a letter. If you've got a beef with coverage, offer kudos first; then share your ideas about how the media might have done a better job, such as using updated terminology and real actors with disabilities! When major media don't cover disability, ask *why?* Don't get nasty. Would you support someone's cause after a nasty encounter? Doubtful, right? Never forget that we are at the *beginning* of a civil rights movement, and many people still don't get what the fuss is all about. Be patient. All of us who care about special needs must represent the population we serve well.

Don't take your responsibility lightly. Help further the cause! Now it's time to enter some pretty emotional territory. So let's turn to Chapter Seven and figure out how we can create a new definition of family and all that it entails . . .

PART THREE

FOCUSING ON THE FAMILY

JUDY WINTER'S
SPECIAL NEEDS BILL OF RIGHTS
FOR SIBLINGS

You have the right to

- Be treated with dignity and respect
- Celebrate your sibling's birth
- Grieve the loss of a sibling without special needs
- Have your needs met, too
- Question excessive child care demands
- Pursue your dreams
- Ask for the support you need, including professional counseling
- Be proud of your sibling's accomplishments—and your own
- Feel protective toward your sibling
- Be able to cry and to feel angry and sad
- Ask tough questions, including *Why?*

7

EMBRACING A NEW DEFINITION OF FAMILY AND PLANNING FOR THE FUTURE

The opposite of love is not hate, but indifference.

—Eli Wiesel

We have spent a lot of time addressing important societal issues affecting the lives of children with special needs, including good programs and services, inclusive education, and the law. We now turn our focus to some emotional issues that strike even closer to home—the subject of family.

We will talk about redefining family, asking for the family support you need (no easy task), and recognizing the valuable roles that fathers and grandparents play in the lives of our children. We will learn how to reclaim leisure time (and put some much-needed fun back into your lives), before briefly addressing the importance of wills and guardianships.

We begin with the story of a family challenged to its parenting core. Special needs parenting success isn't always measured in terms of happy endings. Sometimes we are faced with gut-wrenching decisions that affect the health and welfare of the entire family.

This is a story about a couple who were forced to redefine family—and make tough decisions to seek outside placement for two of their three children.

A SUCCESS STORY

One of the most heart-wrenching decisions that the loving parents of a child with special needs will ever face is whether or not to place their child in a living situation outside their home. Such decisions are often made when a family can no longer effectively meet a child's needs at home—no matter how strong their family commitment.

Parents who choose outside placement for their children due to health and addiction issues, serious financial concerns, or the challenging, complex needs of a child often face the unwarranted, harsh judgment of others. These parents may already feel grief, guilt, and anger about their decision, no matter how right the choice.

It is not our place to judge other families. Sometimes this is the best decision for a family and child. And few parents make it lightly.

Ralph and Bonnie Rennaker faced a group-home placement decision for their two daughters with a rare disorder called MPS III (also called Sanfilippo Syndrome). Their son, Chip, is free of the disorder and has three healthy sons.

According to Barbara Wedehase, MSW, CGC, executive director of the National MPS Society, MPS III is a progressive, neurological, genetic disorder caused by the body's inability to produce enzymes required to break down glycosaminoglycan (GAGs). The resulting buildup of this complex sugar causes damage throughout the body, including the heart, respiratory system, bones and joints, and central nervous system.

Signs of MPS III include an enlarged liver, excess body hair, slow development, breathing problems, toileting problems, hernias, and difficulty with balance. Hearing, speech, and eating challenges may also occur. Because of the neurological base of the disorder, many children develop seizures. These children often exhibit extreme behaviors.

At age three, Jill Rennaker became increasingly hyperactive and could empty the contents of the refrigerator in record time.

Ralph Rennaker recalls a terrifying moment when Jill bolted reck-lessly into the street. "She brushed off a car and spun into my arms unharmed," he recalls. The inability to sleep is also common and often begins in infancy. "I remember sleeping in the girls' bedroom with my head against the door because they were up all night," Ralph Rennaker says.

Wedehase says the behavior challenges of children with MPS III are tough for many families to handle—and parents are often unfairly blamed for them. Bonnie was asked by a psychologist to recall a childhood trauma that may have caused her daughters' behaviors. "I was angry that I even had to address this," she says. "I knew we were excellent parents."

There are four types of MPS III, but the physical characteristics and problems associated with each type are similar. "Each one is caused by the deficiency of a different enzyme," Wedehase says. "But the severity of the disorder is based upon the mutation within the gene."

MPS III occurs in one in seventy thousand births in the United States. There is no cure, only treatment for the medical conditions that result. Life expectancy varies—and the chance of having a sec-ond child with MPS III is one in four.

A Michigan State University physician made Jill's initial diag-nosis when she was nine. Extensive blood and skin tests at the Uni-versity of Michigan confirmed the diagnosis. "Our whole world fell apart," Bonnie says.

Mindy was born seventeen months after Jill. When she became increasingly withdrawn, her parents blamed her sister's behavior; but it was also MPS III.

Wedehase says that early diagnosis of MPS III is often difficult. "These children don't have the characteristic facial features as with other disorders, so they may not look like they have a problem." MPS III is detected by first using a urine screening test. If positive, a blood or skin biopsy must be taken.

For thirteen long years, the Rennakers fought to keep their fam-ily together. They faced years of in-home respite workers who refused to return. And outside placements they call every parent's nightmare. The decision to place their children in a group home was tough. "We did what we could to make our lives— especially Chip's—as normal as possible," Ralph Rennaker says. "But we were merely existing."

Jill and Mindy are now in their thirties—rare for those with MPS III. The disorder has robbed them of their ability to walk or feed themselves, and they are at increased risk for pneumonia. During weekly visits, Ralph and Bonnie Rennaker hold and comfort their daughters much as they did when they were infants.

Chip Rennaker says that his parents' carefully thought-out decisions affected his life positively. "It's important for parents of children with special needs to realize that other children in the family also need attention," he stresses. "The only way a child can get through this and succeed in life is if parents handle it well—and my parents did a very good job of that."

Many parents struggle to find suitable out-of-home placements for their children, even with the assistance of state agencies. Once that placement has been made, the Rennakers say, parents should remain vigilant in overseeing the placement and ensuring that their child is in a safe, healthy environment. Jill and Mindy are fortunate to reside together in a nurturing, family-like environment. "The staff is wonderful and I know our girls are getting excellent care," Bonnie says.

"My parents should be pinned with a Purple Heart for their parenting efforts over the years," Chip adds. "They are wonderful people."

The Rennakers offer words of wisdom for other families facing the issue of outside placement and the demands of special needs. "These are your kids and you have a responsibility to get what's best for them no matter what," Ralph says. "Don't be a tyrant, but don't let anyone ever intimidate you," he says. "If a situation doesn't feel right, shop around."

"And don't *ever* walk away," Bonnie adds . . .

BARBARA WEDEHASE'S TIPS

Coping with MPS III

Barbara Wedehase offers some strategies for families of children with MPS III:

- *Get your child an audiology evaluation.* Children with MPS III are prone to ear infections and hearing loss. If a hearing aid is needed, Wedehase says it will be easier to introduce one early in a child's life.

- *Get a respiratory sleep study at an early age to use as a baseline.* Get your child regular cardiac evaluations from an early age.

- *Set up a safe room in your house.* Put a Dutch door on this room so the bottom half stays closed, but the child can still see that someone is nearby. Provide consistency in routine and avoid excessive stimulation.

- *Put Plexiglas in the windows and put the TV/VCR/DVD up high.* Include soft chew toys. "Children with MPS III do lots of chewing for self-stimulation, and this beats chewing on their fingers. Families become very innovative in addressing MPS III." Wedehase adds, "They may not have control over progression of the disorder, but they do have control over the basic treatments."

- *Parents need to know that research is being conducted, and that advances in medical care can help improve the quality of life for a child with MPS III.* "These parents will go to great lengths to make sure their children are comfortable. They know they won't have their children forever, so they just try to appreciate them every day."

- *Finally, parents should look at the developmental age of their child rather than the chronological age.* "Parents may feel

(continued on next page)

(continued from previous page)

guilty about their child's behavior because they think it means that they are ineffective parents. They need to understand that behavioral conditioning doesn't work for these children, because MPS III is a neurological disorder." For more information, contact the National MPS Society: www.mpssociety.org.

The Rennakers' story is a powerful reminder of the challenges facing many families of children with special needs—and of the importance of asking for help when you need it most. That is one part of responsible parenting. Now let's see how you can better include family members in helping you meet your own special needs parenting challenges.

But first, we need to redefine the term *family*.

Redefining Family

Up to this point in *Breakthrough Parenting for Children with Special Needs*, we have focused most of our attention on recognizing outstanding family members who help their children have better lives.

Unfortunately, not all children will get their needs met by immediate family members—for whatever reason. So I've redefined family to include those adults who help us carry the special needs parenting load, including the staff at the group home where the Rennakers' children now reside.

When it comes to raising children with special needs, the ancient African proverb "*It takes a village to raise a child*" never rang truer.

Lots of good folks contributed their time and talent to help my son maximize his potential. I've even called Eric the *community's child*. No matter how great our parenting efforts were (and I think they were pretty darn terrific!), it would have been really tough for our family to achieve all we did for Eric without the support of some wonderful people outside our immediate family—that's a humbling fact.

We need to remember to honor the everyday heroes in our lives—friends and others, including professionals, who go above and beyond the call of duty, not because they have to but because they care about kids and families. These exceptional individuals go to bat for us and our kids. They deserve our recognition and our heartfelt thanks. Remember to acknowledge them.

Being a child's hero goes beyond terminology and turf.

 DID YOU KNOW?

Intellectual disability is now more acceptable terminology than *mental retardation* or *mentally retarded* (in part due to the continued derogatory use of the term *retard(ed)* by the general public). In 2005, this term represents the most recent change in the language—and has been adopted by Special Olympics and the federal government.

Asking for Family Support

I've been writing about special needs parenting since 1990. Other than education and professional arrogance, no topic has generated as much response to my work as *family*. Many parents have shared with me how disappointed they are because their relatives refused to offer their support, acceptance, and understanding of their parenting situations. This frustrating reality led me to redefine family a long time ago.

I've discovered that some of the best support our kids will ever have may come from those who aren't blood relatives.

Many people are still not comfortable around those with special needs. If you had differences with family members prior to special needs, those disagreements may now intensify and become more complicated—that's a reality you face.

My advice to parents is to stop placing all their family expectations in one basket (unless you want to be really disappointed). By broadening the definition of family, the rewards and support you receive from nonfamily members may prove more fulfilling and supportive than you ever imagined possible. Try it and see!

Here are a few strategies to help parents encourage the support of immediate and extended family—we don't want to let Aunt Mabel and Uncle Fred off the family hook too easily, now do we?

- *Communication is key.* Sound familiar? Your ability to practice good communication skills (including being a good listener) is again being called into play. Effective communication can go a long way toward resolving family issues—before they get out of hand.

- *Arrange regular family meetings.* This is a great opportunity to discuss what's going on in your child's life and how family can support you with any challenges. It's also a super time to include family in any upcoming hospitalizations (time for meal delivery and hospital visits!). Address any concerns you have with the way your family interacts with your child. Be honest, but gracious. Let family members know how much their support means to you and how tough your parenting role can be. Don't sugarcoat it. Take time to hear and address their concerns, too. Focus on needs—not emotions. Embrace a *new* definition of family. This bears repeating: recognize the value of inviting people outside your immediate family whom you like, trust, and admire to serve as support systems. Invite them to family meetings if it's appropriate.

- *Set clear expectations.* What do you want, need, and expect of your family members? How can they best help you with your challenges today? (Charity really *does* begin in the home.) Is there anything that people are doing or saying regarding your child that you cannot and will not tolerate? Share your hopes and dreams and goals for your child. This is time to state clearly what you expect of others. If you don't say it, don't expect it to happen. Offer the training required for family members to become increasingly comfortable interacting with or taking responsibility for your child. This could lead to baby-sitting and overnight stays!

• *Look outside the family for regular daily support.* Don't expect family members to fill ongoing needs for baby-sitting, respite, and the like. They've got responsibilities, too. Access agencies that assist with respite services or hire competent, trained teens or college kids.

• *Work to include your child with special needs in family activities.* Plan ahead for those activities and modifications required to successfully include your child in family outings and activities. This way, *all* of the kids are included.

• *Practice forgiveness whenever possible.* Remember, you are a teacher to others, and advocacy is now a big part of your life. Be patient with family members as you help bring them up to speed about special needs.

• *Make other plans for how and where you spend your time.* If despite all your hard work and best efforts, your family continues to be insensitive to your child's needs (and *yours*), make another choice about when and if you will visit. Don't make excuses for the continued, unacceptable, selfish behavior of family members! Your child deserves better and so do you. It's OK not to go home for the holidays. Cook your own Thanksgiving turkey—and enjoy it in the company of good friends.

To all those family members who are now yelling at me, "But we don't know what to do or what to say! They never ask for our help! They seem to be doing just fine!" Here are five key tips to help take away some of your excuses for inaction:

• *Honor the child's birth and remember his or her birthday.* There is never an excuse good enough for actions and words that make parents think you believe their child's life is less valuable than a child without special needs. Honor this child's birth as you would any other—they are now family.

- *Attend family meetings*. Listen carefully to what's being said, then see where you can help out and sign up for duty. Don't judge. Try to be more compassionate. Unless you've walked in these shoes, you can't possibly understand what it's like living with this parenting demand.

- *Don't ignore children with special needs at family gatherings*. Interact with them and teach your children to do the same. If you aren't sure what to do or say, ask. It's OK to do this. You are all family—remember? If a child can't easily get down the stairs, plan kids' activities upstairs and talk to your children about how to involve their relatives ahead of time. Be a positive role model and example for other family members.

- *Purchase age-appropriate gifts, and use age-appropriate language*. Don't assume that because a child has certain needs, he shouldn't have age-appropriate toys, for example. If you aren't sure, ask. Talk baby talk only to babies.

- *Offer to do child care, bring a meal, send a card, or visit the hospital*. If a child with special needs is in the hospital, stay in the hospital room while the parents get dinner, or just stop by to say hello to break up the monotony of the day. Share a hug and your support.

- *Put yourself in the challenging parenting shoes of your family member*. Maybe you are lucky that this is not your parenting reality (maybe not). But why not share the responsibilities once and a while? Don't pretend this family challenge doesn't exist and refuse to address it. That really *hurts*. Even the smallest support or encouragement can be a blessing to families of children with special needs. An hour to you is like a weekend to these family members. If the parenting roles were reversed, how would you want to be treated or supported? *Is what you are doing good enough?* Up your family game! Disability can happen to anyone at any time. Be sensitive to that reality. Keep trying to find ways that you can help support other family members through your own actions.

- *Don't make simplistic religious comments no matter how well intentioned.* Statements like "God never gives you more than you can handle," or "God chose you to raise this child because you are special," or other such remarks are *not* comforting to most parents. Please refrain. But be willing to listen to a parent's take (and possibly strong opinions) on the subject.

- *Finally, please, watch your language, and please raise your expectations.* Please watch your tone and lower your voice, too. Review other tips in this book for further help.

CELEBRATING FATHERS AND GRANDPARENTS

I need to shout out some loud kudos for great dads and loving grandparents everywhere! Dads are often unfairly undervalued and overlooked in the important parenting equation by society. And the selfless and supportive role many grandparents play in our children's lives often goes unrecognized.

Did you know that more grandparents than ever before are stepping up to the parenting plate to help raise their grandchildren—when they could be *coasting* into the golden years.

Bless you all!

A Personal Story: Eric's Grandma

Grandma Mary is a gem.

Her real name is Mary Jane Pressley Winter, but *grandma* suits her fine. Mary is what a grandma should be—kind and gentle and always smiling. She proudly boasts eight grandchildren but never claims a favorite, at least not aloud.

When her visions of a perfect grandson were shattered with the diagnosis of Eric's cerebral palsy in 1990, my mother-in-law quickly rearranged her thinking, and her heart, to fit with the new reality—and did so with amazing grace.

Little has been written about the grief that families of children with special needs endure. Even less is said of the anguish experienced by grandparents eagerly anticipating the renewed joys of parenting, minus its demands. Their visions of "perfect" newborns are often replaced by neonatal intensive care visits. Instead of cigars, stuffed animals, and back slapping, they face the hum of medical intervention, fragile infants, and broken dreams. The experience can prove overwhelming.

For many family members, the birth of a special child represents the death of a dream—but not so for Grandma Mary. She enthusiastically claimed her grandson. It was she who lovingly rocked Eric, with life-sustaining tubes connected to his body. Her gentle ways offered healing that rivaled the best medical treatment, aiding in Eric's recovery and ours. She never doubted his value—or her role.

When others seemed insensitive to the magnitude of our parenting challenges, Grandma Mary was busy adding a wheelchair ramp to her front porch to ensure Eric's weekly visits. They were best buddies, who loved playing the guitar, reading chapter books, baking cookies, and traveling together.

Mary and I know that a priceless piece of her heart will always belong to that one special grandson in a wheelchair. Their sacred bond blessed us all . . .

JUDY WINTER'S TIPS

Grandparents

There are many ways that you can contribute to caring for your grandson or granddaughter with special needs. Here are a few ideas to get you started.

- *Get involved.* Most children with special needs aren't nearly as fragile as people think they are. Don't be afraid to interact with them. You won't *break* them. (If you do, be sure to let me know!) The time you spend with your grandchildren can be rewarding for you both. Don't miss out on it.

- *Be a great example for other family members.* Be willing to challenge family members who fail to support your son or daughter and your grandchild. Make waves! Grandparents are important child advocates, too.

- *Set clear limits.* Make it clear which responsibilities you do and do not feel comfortable accepting. If lifting a child into a wheelchair or handling aggressive behavior is too rough for you, say so. Talk about what you *can* do with your grandchild, such as read a favorite book, make cookies, go to the zoo together, color Easter eggs, or talk on the phone. It's very important that you connect with that grandchild on a regular basis, as you would with any other grandchild. (You *are* connecting with your grandchildren, right?)

- *Be careful not to overstep your role.* Most parents of children with special needs are in need of your support and love, not your criticism and judgment. Be a positive, supportive force in your children's lives. Chances are, if you haven't had a child with special needs, your parenting expertise may not be all that you think it is. Be sensitive about giving unsolicited parenting advice.

- *Network with other grandparents with or without special needs concerns.* If you have peers who have great relationships with their grandchildren, talk to them about their success. What tips do they have for *you* to make your role with your grandchildren more successful and rewarding?

- *Seek out professional support.* If you are struggling with your own grief at having a grandchild with special needs, seek out appropriate support, including groups specifically for grandparents. It's OK, and sometimes necessary, to do this.

Now let's take time to celebrate all those amazing dads by using another one of my family members as an example—just to let you know that we practice what *I* preach.

A Personal Story: Eric's Dad

My husband, Dick, is a certified public accountant (CPA). He's rock steady and balances out the journalist gypsy in me. After your world is ripped apart with the reality of special needs, parenting roles and expectations get redefined. A mom hoping for a ballerina may never get to buy toe shoes and satin ribbons. And a dad dreaming of a star pitcher may watch those baseball games from handicapped seating.

Eric's dad has coached youth softball and has run marathons, so I know he grieved the loss of a son who couldn't play catch, ride a bike, or say Daddy. But he didn't love Eric any less, and not once did he measure Eric's worth in terms of MVP awards or future athletic scholarships. He measured gains in terms of improved motor skills, increased physical stamina, growing speech, and being able to spend Saturdays together doing guy stuff—like going to Home Depot and buying light bulbs!

I used to love sneaking up on my boys as they shared favorite bedtime stories. I spied on them—enchanted, as Dick used that soft voice reserved for the moments when, free of male expectations, he would nuzzle his son's silky hair, completely absorbed in fatherhood. I used to watch nervously as he threw Eric giggling into the air and called him "tough guy." And when Dick took Eric on his cherished morning jogs, I would stare out the window long after they'd disappeared from sight.

My husband always looked beyond disability to connect solidly with the son he adored. He always makes time for our daughter, Jenna, too and has supported her in many ways.

I remember smiling every single time he yelled her name loudly at competitive cheerleading events in high school and recall track meets where I stood back, camera ready, savoring the exact moment when Dick proudly cheered Jenna over the finish line. More recently, he drove her across the country so she could realize her dream of attending college in Southern California.

Years ago, when I asked Jenna what she most loved about her dad, she said, "He's always there for me and he treats Eric just like any other kid."

This is one father who has always understood his important role as *dad* in both of his children's lives, no matter what curve balls life has thrown his way.

You can do the same.

JUDY WINTER'S TIPS

Dads

Here are some tips just for all you dads out there!

- *Work as a team with your child's mother.* Come to agreements on such issues as discipline, medical treatments, and inclusion. Let *your* voice be heard, too.

- *If you are divorced, put aside your differences and emotions.* Work as a unified parenting team to be more successful in meeting your child's needs.

- *Take turns taking your child to appointments and school.* Get to know team members, your child's routine, likes and dislikes. If the only parent most people see is a child's mom (because you haven't been involved), it will be tougher for you to gain parenting respect from others— and that of your children.

- *Help your child with homework.* There's plenty of that to go around.

- *Give your child's mother the gift of time away.* This is especially important if she is the primary caretaker during the week. This is a great way to bond with your child.

(*continued on next page*)

(continued from previous page)

- *Take a hard look at your expectations for your child and create new ones.* A wheelchair user may not run a race or play ball in the traditional way, but he can participate in sports with your help and support. Be extra careful not to let your child pay the price of your disappointment and anger. Deal with it!

- *Step up to the parenting plate.* Raising this child is your responsibility, too. Be a positive role model that you and your children can be proud of.

Reclaiming Leisure Time

Leisure time includes those activities that are a regular part of the lives of most families, like going on vacations, eating out on Friday nights, and going to the movies. Having a healthy family life means adding these components back into your lives, including for the sake of siblings. More about them in Chapter Nine.

Depending on your child's needs, doing this can be quite challenging—but rarely impossible. Modify and accommodate activities as needed, but work hard not to shut them out of your life completely.

Early in his life, my son was very sensitive to noise and touch. No big surprise given his medical needs. During those earliest years, Eric would barely tolerate us stopping the van long enough to make it through the drive-thru at McDonald's to order a Big Mac and fries. We had to keep moving!

Or let the wailing begin . . .

We began adding fun back into our lives very slowly, and we did not give up. It took lots of determination for us to stay with it. But each time we did, Eric's tolerance, and our leisure time, increased. Little by little, our son got used to noise and crowds, and we claimed more fun family times. You don't know what's possible with your child unless you try. Each small step may lead to the next success.

Before his death, Eric could out-shop me at the mall (no easy task), and he loved spending leisurely time in bookstore cafés people-watching. He loved going to popular music concerts (especially if guitars were involved). We would arrange for him to sit up close so he could see, which was critical to success with this venue. Then we would carry his manual wheelchair down flights of stairs to claim our seats.

I still remember the night that Eric sat mesmerized by the opening act, before one of his earliest musical heroes, Mary Chapin Carpenter, took to the stage. I knew then we had come a long way.

Eric also loved to travel. He flew to Florida and rode ferry boats to Mackinac Island (one of our favorite destinations) and "ran" their Eight-Mile–Island Race in his wheelchair (and got a medal!). The summer before he died, Eric jumped waves with his dad at Lake Michigan like all the other kids. I could not have envisioned these great adventures early on.

We just wanted to go to McDonald's for fries . . .

These outings took innovative thought, careful planning, bull-dog determination, and a great love for our son. We had to think outside the parenting box many times.

Leisure time is important to all families. Put *fun* back in your lives. You may need to modify your plans and pack lots of extra supplies. Your family vehicle may threaten to break under the weight of all the stuff, but it's worth the effort. By risking new adventures, we got a big chunk of our lives back—plus some priceless memories.

 ## JUDY WINTER'S TIPS
Leisure Time

Leisure time helps balance all those challenging parenting moments—now go out and have some family fun:

- *Go to the movies.* If your child's behavior is of concern, go to the movies at less popular times. Pick movies you

(continued on next page)

(continued from previous page)

think your child will like. You will be more successful if your child is already interested in the subject appearing on the screen. Build on each small success. If you can only stay for fifteen minutes the first time, fine. Try for thirty minutes the next time—until you are watching the end of the movie. I was amazed—and very happy—when this finally happened with my son! Sit where you can get up and leave easily if needed. Allow older siblings to take a friend and sit wherever *they* want.

- *Take vacations and road trips.* If you're going on any kind of an escape, make sure you know where the emergency facilities are, check on accessibility, and pack a *travel bag* with all the supplies your child needs. Then repack the bag when you get home so it's ready to go for the next quick trip.

- *Eat out.* Ask for corner tables with lots of room and privacy, especially if you hate staring. If behavior's a concern, choose family-friendly places with lots of kids. This is no time to be trying out four-star restaurants (maybe down the road), and remember, you can always sit outside at McDonald's on a warm summer night or picnic in the backyard and star gaze. *Ahh, life's simple pleasures!*

- *Make the most of your weekends.* Go to the zoo, park, church, water park, or amusement park (Eric rode a roller coaster!), or take a walk. You don't have to go far from home or spend a lot of money to have the experience of *getting away.* Plan outings with other families of children with special needs. There is support in numbers—especially when you are new to this parenting challenge.

- *Capture the moments.* Keep a scrapbook, take photos, and videotape so you can relive your adventures during those times when it's tougher to get out. Looking back to see

> how far you have come can be a great motivator and
> raise your spirits. I will be forever grateful for all the sum-
> mer adventures we captured on camera and film. They
> help us relive family moments and realize what a great
> life Eric had in light of his challenges.

Because we took the risks and brought many leisure activities
back into our lives, our family has no regrets—we only wish that we
could have had more time with Eric to create additional family
memories. *Treasure leisure time with your family.*

 DID YOU KNOW?

For seventy-five years, the Shriners of North America
(http://www.shrinershq.org/index.html) have been operating
specialized hospitals nationwide that treat children up to age
eighteen with orthopedic problems, burns, and spinal-cord
injuries: free of charge! Check it out!

PLANNING FOR THE FUTURE

My husband and I once lived dangerously on the edge. We had no
will (sound familiar?) and no clue as to who would be willing to
raise a teenager and a child with physical needs should we meet an
untimely death from doing something incredibly impulsive (and
stupid), like bungee jumping!

As we traveled out of town one day to a writer's conference held
in the tropical paradise of Maui, I knew we needed to put our legal
affairs in order—and pronto.

What if our plane crashed (or we refused to come home)? I
could see the headlines: "Bad parents leave two darling children
(and a power wheelchair) homeless—film at 11:00!"

I'm joking about a serious subject. Most of us don't like to think
about plane crashes, fatal car accidents, or other life traumas. But

by not planning for "what if?" we leave our children's futures at risk—and their lives are complicated enough.

Do you really want to leave important decisions about your child's life up to the state (the answer should be "Absolutely not!") or to some relatives you hardly know? I didn't think so. Consider this one more area in which you must become an advocate.

With the help of some great information shared by Marla Kraus, executive director of the nonprofit organization Special Needs Advocate for Parents (SNAP) (Snapinfo.org), I'll try to make this subject as painless for you as possible, while further empowering you.

According to Kraus, an attorney and parent, SNAP's mission is to improve the quality of life for children of all ages with special needs and their parents or caregivers by serving as a resource providing information, education, advocacy, and referrals, regardless of age or disability.

That means helping them address all that unnerving legal stuff they'd rather avoid, like trusts and wills, guardianships and conservatorships, and issues with medical insurance. SNAP's Medical Insurance Empowerment Program helps parents figure out how to maximize insurance benefits for their children.

Their services also include the Information and Advocacy Program, Special Needs Estate Planning Resource Center, and the quarterly newsletter the *Snap Report*. SNAP is worth checking out.

Kraus advises families to have the following four things in place to protect children with special needs. And remember, when it comes to the legal issues addressed in *Breakthrough Parenting for Children with Special Needs*, all those rules and regulations and legal lingo may vary. So please check your own state's guidelines.

- *Make a will.* Kraus says everybody should have one. "If you don't have a will, you don't get to express your own desires. The state will decide for you!"
- *Give your choices careful thought.* Address issues of guardianships and conservatorships. Kraus says that guardianships usually apply to children under age eighteen, and conservatorships tend to

apply to adults over age eighteen with special needs and vary from state to state. Ask yourself who's going to care for your child if and when you aren't here. Do you see your child living on his or her own? Does your child need a guardian? If so, approach people you are interested in and ask them if they will accept this responsibility. Make sure they fully understand what they are agreeing to take on.

- *Write a letter of intent.* Kraus says this isn't a legal document but rather expresses *your intentions for your child* in writing. It should include all the different areas of importance to the quality of your child's life, from detailed medical issues, to a child's daily routine, to names of professionals who work with your child, to religious preferences, to a child's favorite movies and televisions shows and pizza toppings, to the hospital you prefer or the medications your child must take. Kraus advises each parent to write his or her own part of the letter of intent because they are often responsible for different areas of the child's life. "It's illuminating for each parent to see the other's viewpoint," Kraus says. She adds that writing this document can be a daunting task, but an important one. She advises parents not to get discouraged and to make the document as long as it needs to be, and then update it often. "If it matters to the quality of your child's life, then put it in there."

- *Consider establishing a special needs trust.* "Parents need to ask how they are going to provide (fund) the resources required to ensure the quality of life they want for their child after they are gone." Kraus says this trust is an estate-planning tool created by Congress to allow families a place to put money for covering costs of supplemental care over those of food, clothing, and shelter—things typically covered under Supplemental Security Income (SSI). It's sometimes called a *supplemental trust* and can be created in a will or can stand alone. This trust may cover the costs of such things as special therapies, vacations, or nursing homes. Assets can include money, houses, or cars. Medical malpractice awards can go into this type of trust. Parents can buy life insurance so there is money to go into the trust to provide for their child's care after they are gone. Family members can contribute to this trust.

DID YOU KNOW?

Marla Kraus, executive director of SNAP and an attorney, says that wills, guardianships, conservatorships, and special needs trusts are legal issues that require the involvement of an attorney. She stresses the importance of working with a financial-planning expert in the field of special needs. "Sometimes a lawyer will draft the trust, for example, but they won't assist parents in figuring out how to fund it," she says, "which makes it basically useless." For more information, visit www.snap info.org.

Plan well to ensure your child's best future—and your own peace of mind.

SPECIAL TIPS

If you have been reading this book cover to cover, you have taken in a ton of knowledge and food for parenting thought. So let's take a brief break to honor your efforts with this one key tip—and give you a chance to catch your breath!

Take a few minutes to see just how far you have come. Recognize your important efforts to become an increasingly empowered parent. (I knew you could do this!) Doesn't it feel good? Now take some time to reward your hard work in meaningful ways—before we move on to the final chapters of this book. You have now been exposed to a wealth of parenting knowledge that took me fifteen years to acquire (and digest). Use this information well—and make yourself and your children proud.

Special Resources

Here are a number of resources that can provide you with even more helpful information. Your list of support just keeps on growing . . .

Adoption

- The National Adoption Center (NAC): www.adopt.org.
- National Foster Parent Association (NPA): http://www.nfpainc.org.
- National Adoption Information Clearinghouse (NAIC)/ U.S. Dept. of Health and Human Services Administration for Children and Families (many links!): http://naic.acf.hhs.gov.
- *Adopting the Hurt Child: Hope for Families with Special-Needs Kids: A Guide for Parents and Professionals*, by Gregory C. Keck and Regina M. Kupecky.

Fathers

- The Fathers Network: www.fathersnetwork.org.
- www.Fathers.com: includes link to National Center for Fathering (NCF).
- www.fatherhood.org.

Grandparents

- AARP: Caring for your Grandchild: www.aarp.org.
- Parents Advocacy Coalition for Educational Rights (PACER): www.Pacer.org: offers grandparent-to-grandparent resources for special needs.

Planning for the Future

- Special Needs Advocate for Parents (SNAP): www.snap info.org (888-310-9889). SNAP partners with MetLife.com. Marla Kraus, executive director: mkraus@snapinfo.org.
- *Making Plans, A Financial Guide for People with Down Syndrome and Their Families*, by the National Down Syndrome Society: www.ndss.org.

- *With Open Arms, Embracing a Bright Financial Future for You and Your Child*, by Easter Seals: www.easterseals.com.

- *Laying Community Foundation for Your Child with a Disability: How to Establish Relationships That Will Support Your Child After You're Gone*, by Linda J. Stengle.

- *Planning for Children with Special Needs*, MetLife Division of Estate Planning for Special Kids: MetDesk: www.metlife.com.

- *Planning for the Future: Providing a Meaningful Life for a Child with a Disability After Your Death*, by Arnold E. Grant and L. Mark Russell.

Travel

- *Barrier-Free Travel: A Nuts and Bolts Guide for Wheelers and Slow Walkers*, by Candy Harrington.

- *Great American Vacations for Travelers with Disabilities: With Complete Accessibility Information on Hotels, Restaurants and Attractions* (2nd ed.), a Fodor's vacation planner.

Genetic Disorders and Other Medical Conditions

- Alliance of Genetic Support Groups: www.geneticalliance.org.

- The National MPS Society: www.mpssociety.org: provides numerous booklets and helpful information for families through their online library.

- National Organization of Rare Diseases: www.rarediseases.org.

- Little People of America, Inc.: www.lpaonline.org.

- Children's Miracle Network (CMN): www.cmn.org.

- American Association of People with Disabilities (AAPD): http://www.aapd-dc.org.

- European Disability Forum (EDF): http://www.edf-feph.org.
- *Tongue Fu! How to Deflect, Disarm, and Defuse Any Verbal Conflict*, by Sam Horn.

Special Note

The language used to identify specific special needs continues to change. As of 2005, here are some examples of *people-first* language, which you should use to address special needs—thanks to Gail Williamson (DSALA.org), our success story in Chapter Six. Keep updated on current terminology, use it, and challenge others to use it, too.

Remember to use people-first language—always!

- Person who has *quadriplegia*, not a quad.
- Person who is *mobility impaired*.
- Person with *cerebral palsy*, not C.P. kid.
- Person who is on *crutches*, not (derogatory) person on sticks.
- Person who has *mental illness*, not insane person.
- Person who has *leg* or *arm amputation*, not leg or arm amputee.
- Person with a *disability*, not disabled or handicapped person.
- Person who is a *wheelchair user*, not wheelchair bound or confined to a wheelchair.
- Person who is *blind* or *visually impaired*, not blind person or vision-impaired person.
- Person who is *short statured*, *little person*, or *person who has dwarfism*, never midget and not dwarf.
- Person who has *Down syndrome*, not Down's kid or Mongoloid.
- Person with a *brain injury*, please don't say brain-dead (my addition!).

Now let's continue our discussion of *family* by turning to Chapter Eight and adding marriage, self-care, faith, and forgiveness and avoiding the danger of adding vices to the empowerment mix. We will also address the most devastating parenting blow of all—the death of a child.

8

PRESERVING YOUR MARRIAGE, CARING FOR YOURSELF, AND SURVIVING THE DEATH OF A CHILD

Humor makes all things tolerable.

—Henry Ward Beecher

Most parents of children with special needs are so busy advocating for their children on the educational, medical, and societal fronts, they often neglect their own needs. But special needs parenting is a lot like running a marathon: without the proper training, you may be at increased risk for parenting burnout.

The fact is, it's nearly impossible to continue to meet the needs of any child, much less a child with special needs, if you don't feed your own body, mind, and spirit—your life is about more than just special needs.

The information in this chapter was chosen to help you remedy what's ailing you or at the very least make you start talking about it. It's pretty darn difficult to raise a healthy, productive, independent child if your own personal life is in shambles.

We are our children's most important role models. Let's see how we can make things better for you on the home front by talking about such important topics as preserving your marriage, caring for yourself, avoiding hidden vices, practicing faith and forgiveness, maintaining your sense of humor, and facing the death of a child.

We begin with an upbeat story about a pretty cool guy living large in light of being diagnosed with a disability, not once, but twice in his lifetime. He's got a college degree, solid career, a great sense of humor—and a healthy marriage of eighteen years.

A SUCCESS STORY

It's easy to forget that Al Swain is blind—and a wheelchair user. The energetic, forty-seven-year-old associate director of the Capital Area Center for Independent Living provides leadership, motivation, and vital resources to Michigan residents with special needs. Swain's job is to help his clients access such vital and limited community resources as housing, employment, skills training, and peer support groups. That's no easy feat.

Swain is one of Michigan's leading disability rights advocates and serves on the Michigan Disability Rights Coalition and the Michigan Commission on Disability Concerns. An international speaker, Swain recently spoke at Bermuda's Accessibility Awareness Week, where his discussions with top cabinet officials led to a bill similar to the Americans with Disabilities Act being introduced into Parliament.

"When I think of who I am, disability is not the first thing that pops into my head," Swain says. "Having special needs is only part of who I am."

He was only nine years old when undiagnosed multiple sclerosis (MS) ravaged his optic nerve. Within three months, Swain went from being an active third grader with 20/20 vision to a young boy facing total blindness.

According to Arney Rosenblat, public affairs director for the National Multiple Sclerosis Society, MS is an unpredictable, lifelong neurological disease in which the body's overactive immune system misidentifies its own tissue as an infection and then turns on itself. Symptoms range from numbness and tingling, double vision and blindness, to vertigo, slurred speech, extreme fatigue, and complete paralysis. Symptoms may come and go.

"The hallmark of MS is unpredictability," Rosenblat says. "It does not follow a set path from A to Z." It's also tough to diagnose.

Of the estimated four hundred thousand people affected by MS in the United States, at least twenty thousand to twenty-five thousand are under age eighteen. MS is often overlooked in children, people of color, and men. "Men tend to get MS less often than women, but when they do get it, it tends to be more debilitating," Rosenblat explains.

Al Swain didn't know that his own blindness was caused by MS until progression of the disease resulted in having to use a wheelchair by the time he was seventeen.

The symptoms of MS in children are similar to those seen in adults. "A person in our office diagnosed with MS in her twenties was called a klutz as a child. She was always running into things, dropping things, or tripping," Rosenblat says. "Those can be symptoms of MS at a young age. But nobody connected the dots and that often happens."

MS is most often treated with medications to address underlying symptoms and help manage them so people can lead more productive lives. The cause remains unknown. "We are making extraordinary strides in controlling the disease using therapies that intervene with symptoms and slow the progression of the disease," Rosenblat says.

Al Swain exhibits a rock-solid sense of self that transcends disability and race, something he credits to his mom—the single parent of four children—and his biggest cheerleader. His mother recently passed away and Swain never knew his father. "But my mom made me feel valuable and worthwhile as a person," he says. "She gave me the message that I was equal to everyone else. Not better than, and not less than."

After Al Swain became blind, he left his home in Niles, Michigan, to join three hundred others students at what was then called the Michigan School for the Blind—the same school attended by his friend, music legend Stevie Wonder.

Swain's mother recognized early on the importance of giving her son every opportunity to learn how to live well with blindness so he could become an increasingly independent adult. In 1967, when many children with special needs were still being institutionalized, she sent her son to a well-respected school with the staff, training, and resources required to help Swain adjust to blindness— and become a productive, independent, and educated citizen.

This mom and child advocate was ahead of her time.

"As a blind person, one of the best things that happened to me was that I was 120 miles away from home while I was going through the initial transition from seeing to not seeing," he explains. "I think I may have gained some additional independence as a result." Swain thrived in the residential setting and went home on weekends. "The experiences we had were like those that other kids got in any other school in America," Swain says. "The attitude of the supportive staff was, 'You're blind, so what? You need to prepare yourself for life, just like other kids.'"

Swain was valedictorian of his 1974 class and obtained a bachelor's degree in sociology from Olivet College in Olivet, Michigan, which he attended on academic and athletic scholarships.

In recent years, the impact of MS on Swain's fine motor skills has left him unable to read Braille. Swain limits his use of adaptive technology to a Kurzweil Reading Machine, which reads print for him, and a talking watch and alarm clock to keep himself on schedule. He uses a tape recorder to record his daily work activities, which a human reader-assistant then transcribes for the organization's monthly activity reports.

"I'm not a big gadget guy," he admits.

Swain has been married for eighteen years to Rebecca, who is visually impaired (more about their relationship under Preserving Your Marriage). She has a master's degree in English and proofreads Braille textbooks for use in classrooms across the country. They met at a support group. Swain laughs when he says he refused to date women with disabilities in college. "I felt that people were trying to limit my choices."

If he could erase one of his disabilities, he'd reclaim his sight. "I'd like to drive a car instead of depending on public transportation. I'd like to see the faces of my wife, friends, and family members—and my own," he adds. "The visual image I have of myself is from when I was nine. I think that I probably look a little bit different today."

Before Swain's mother passed away, she realized her dreams of seeing her son educated and gainfully employed, the results of the seeds she planted on the day her nine-year-old son first lost his sight. Her unwavering support continued until her death.

Swain may not have had the traditional two-parent household of many children with special needs, but he got what he needed to thrive, in light of his sudden disability.

"My mother taught me that I could do anything," he says.

It was a powerful lesson.

Today Al Swain's life is filled with purpose and meaning because many people believed in his value throughout his life—and refused to *further disable* him. Whatever his mama and others taught him, it stuck!

Let's see what her son has to say about marriage . . .

Preserving Your Marriage

Al and Rebecca Swain have been married for eighteen years. Al says they are both big music lovers, who decided to get married after playing *Name That Tune* at a social event. "That was it!" he jokes. "We both have good senses of humor, come from small town backgrounds, and share similar values and beliefs about why we're here," he says.

In addition to facing the relationship challenges experienced by most married couples, this partnership must also address special needs. "We seem to be compatible and our disabilities seem to mesh," Swain explains. "Because of Rebecca's own visual challenges, we didn't have to develop any level of understanding around disability," Swain explains.

Swain cites fatigue and other health concerns for the couple's decision to remain childless. "Kids have boundless energy and a continuous need for nurturing. If you aren't prepared for that, then you shouldn't have children."

Here are some relationship strategies that Swain offers his clients and practices in his own marriage:

- *Pick your battles.* "Some couples fight about everything, no matter how big or little. Most of the stuff people fight over ain't that big a deal," he says.

- *Take time for each other.* This couple used to check into local hotels for regular romantic overnight getaways. Today they often travel together for speaking engagements. "You don't have to go far away from home to create a change of pace in your life."

- *Put leisure activities in your life.* Be active as a couple. The Swain's live in a four-corner neighborhood where transportation is not an issue, so they can easily walk to a café for lunch or go out for ice cream. "That helps keep us active so we don't feel stuck at home." Swain advises families to seek out respite services. This frees them up so they can have important time away from regular caregiver demands. Swain acknowledges that respite services aren't as available as they should be nationwide (write a letter!). "We need to channel more dollars and energies into respite programs for families," he stresses. He calls respite a two-way break, which kids need as well as adults. "I know that the time I spent away from my family resulted in some good things happening for me."

- *Maintain intimacy.* We aren't just talking about sex here. Swain says that intimacy is a big part of any relationship. "In the past, rehab and other folks didn't see this as important for people with disabilities." Swain calls it important for all couples. "I recently bought a standing wheelchair so I can stand upright and give my wife a full-body hug."

Today many resources address intimacy and adaptations for all couples, including those with disabilities. Here are a few resources to get you started:

- *Sexuality and Disabilities*, edited by Romel W. Mackelprang, DSW, and Deborah Valentine, Ph.D., MSW.
- *Strengthening Relationships*, by Nicolas Martin, M.A.
- Special Needs Project: America's Disability Bookstore: www.specialneeds.com.

After parenting a child with special needs, here's my own simple take on marriage. Most stuff ultimately falls into two categories: *the stuff you can fix* and *the stuff you can't*. Figure out what you can fix and fix it—then let the rest slide and move on.

You've got other things to do with your precious time.

A Word About the D Word (Divorce)

Boy, nothing gets me going as much as parents who refuse to accept their share of the responsibility for bringing a child into this world—unless it's the D word (or educational inequality!).

There will be times when divorce may well be the right decision for a couple to make. That said, I've never forgotten the story a mom shared with me about her husband, who walked out on their special needs situation when their child was a toddler. Her story made me angry. Still does.

This man didn't think he could handle his new reality but decided his wife could. He left her to pick up all the parenting pieces alone, as if raising this child was solely her responsibility. It took a decade of struggle for this woman to recover from this relationship blow and put her life and the life of her child back together, but she did.

Not everyone can.

Be careful about making hasty, lasting relationship decisions as soon as the special needs waters get a little choppy—especially during those early years when you are experiencing shock, denial, and anger and don't have the skills, support, and resources you need to see beyond the scary parenting horizon.

It's easy during these rough moments to think that your life is over and want to do anything to escape the reality (most of us have been there). But your life is *not* over. You are in a big transition phase. For many families, things do improve a lot, with a solid parenting commitment.

Marriage is hard work even without special needs. Forget about all those quickie Vegas celebrity weddings with forty-eight-hour annulments that you see on TV (with no kids involved!). This is one of those *for better or worse* times that define real marriage vows.

Don't bolt from a marriage just because your child has special needs.

If you are struggling in any way, shape, or form—or are thinking about leaving your marriage, seek professional counseling. You may just need someone to talk to. Do everything in your power to try to make the situation work before giving up, unless there's abuse involved—that's deal breaker!

If you think it's tough handling special needs parenting with a partner, try handling it alone. Would *you* want to do this by yourself? I doubt it. Make another choice, for the sake of your family!

JUDY WINTER'S TIPS

Marriage

Try these tips for supporting your marriage:

- *Schedule a date night each week.* You don't have to spend a lot of money. Share coffee or dessert, go to the park or beach, or go grocery shopping together—it's gotta be done and you get to choose your own ice cream and cereal. Time spent together as a couple away from parenting responsibilities can energize you for the week ahead and keep you connected. Such moments help balance out your life.

- *Socialize with other parents of kids with special needs whose company you enjoy.* We discovered a whole new group of great friends, who shared a priceless understanding of our challenging parenting role. Don't ignore these valuable friendships—nurture them. They are irreplaceable.

- *Take care of your appearance.* Taking good care of your appearance feeds your self-esteem, which can help you address parenting challenges with greater confidence. Wear only that clothing that makes you feel good.

- *Seek out respite services and hire baby-sitters.* Many respite programs may have sliding payment scales. Having well-trained support in place is priceless. If your budget makes it hard for you to hire baby-sitters, trade off child care with other families. Do whatever you can to arrange for regular time away from your parenting demands. Respite is a key to good self-care—and good mental health. See pages 196–197 for links to statewide respite resources.

- *Communicate.* There's that word again—you know the drill.

- *Appreciate your differences in parenting style and show your appreciation.* We spend a lot of time telling each other what we are doing wrong. Try to recognize the positive actions and traits of your partner, then *tell* him. Try hard not to criticize each other.

- *Don't expect your partner to meet all your needs.* That's a heavy load for anyone to carry. Work to recognize and meet your own needs.

- *Take turns being "up."* It's great to know that on a really bad day your partner has your back; return the favor. You are in this together.

- *Work as a team.* There's lots of power in being a united front. Don't try to carry the parenting load all by yourself—you risk burning out fast.

(continued on next page)

(continued from previous page)

- *Keep romance alive.* That includes having sex more than once a year.

- *Avoid the danger of hidden vices.* Reaching for alcohol or drugs (*super* dangerous territory), or another person, as well as things like excessive shopping (remember the mortgage payment), gambling, or overeating and downing excessive amounts of caffeine (which saps your precious energy or makes you so wired you can't stop talking) are temporary fixes that will most likely further complicate your life. Avoid them! Special needs parenting requires you to be in the best shape of your life: physically, emotionally, and spiritually. (Just try parenting with a hangover!) Your demands require a higher level of self-discipline than most—leaving little room for self-destructive or selfish, ego-centered behavior. When it comes to special needs, toeing the line (think self-discipline) can make a huge difference.

THE IMPORTANCE OF SELF-CARE

All parents need to take time out to meet their physical, emotional, and spiritual needs—needs that are intensified with special needs. Everyone's needs are different. It's important to figure out what *you* need to deal more productively with your stress load.

Raising children with special needs to reach their full potential is no easy task—all the more reason to take time out.

Here are a few more tips to help you embrace healthy self-care practices.

They may even help you avoid the D word.

- *Take regular time outs.* Most people can benefit from regular opportunities to eat a full meal without interruption or watch a movie from start to finish. Other parents dream of having time alone in their own homes, to take a leisurely bath, to work out, to watch a favorite television program, or to read current magazines and newspapers cover to cover. These actions can help us get back in the parenting ring, instead of getting burned out or feeling hopeless or depressed.

- *Grab some zzzzz's whenever you can.* Most new parents are advised to take naps while their babies are sleeping—with good reason. This is also great advice for parents of children with special needs, who often experience interrupted sleep. I used to fantasize about the luxury of having eight hours of sleep each night. Now that I have it, I keep waking up. The grass always looks greener . . .

- *Use leisure time wisely.* If grandma offers to watch your child, don't mop the floor or wash the dishes. Go shopping, go for a walk, catch up on your sleep, get your hair done, or go to the movies. Escape for a while.

- *Exercise.* Exercise really does help relieve all that parenting stress that can increase your risk of depression, addiction, and even heart disease and other serious illnesses. Go for daily walks as a family. It's good for everybody to get some fresh air and may keep you from feeling stuck at home when you have no child care. Make healthier food choices, too.

THE POWER OF THE THREE F'S: FAITH, FREEDOM, AND FRIENDSHIP

Special needs parenting demands important survival skills. You need superhuman patience, the energy of a triathlete, stellar communication skills, a wicked sense of humor, the ability to juggle finances creatively, a positive attitude in the most infuriating situations, and a huge commitment to seeing a child's potential when all those around you are highlighting every flaw. Man!

No one said your special needs parenting role would be easy (at least I didn't!). It helps to have *faith, freedom,* and *friendship*—three F words you *can* say in public!

Faith

Turning to faith during challenging parenting moments offers you a great opportunity for healing, reflection, and renewal, whatever your spiritual beliefs. Faith allows us to call on a higher power when we feel that we can't possibly take on one more special needs parenting challenge.

Faith keeps you going when you're feeling vulnerable and when you need to vent powerful emotions like grief and anger—without fear of judgment. It allows us to voice our wildest parenting dreams and our deepest grief. It helps us find reason for hope, when others tell us we aren't facing reality (again).

Faith helps us see light on the darkest days. Had I abandoned my faith, my son would have paid a steep price, and so would I. In fact, I doubt I would be talking to you right now. My deeply rooted spiritual beliefs continue to help me heal from my son's untimely and gut-wrenching death. Talk about the potential for having a crisis of faith (which I haven't, yet). But I have yelled a few bad things at God . . .

My advice is to draw strength from your religious or spiritual beliefs; then share those beliefs wisely. This is no time to start preaching salvation to others.

A word about *forgiveness*, that little word that makes most of us wiggle and squirm and get all defensive. Don't underestimate the power of forgiveness to heal your deepest parenting wounds. My advice is to set all those nasty grudges free, once and for all. There's power and freedom in letting that stuff go, no matter how badly you think you've been treated or how unfair you think your life is. (Trust me, someone's life is worse.) The alternative is hanging on and suffering—not so great.

Forgiveness can set you free. Hmmm . . . freedom, personal empowerment, and love, versus a life of self-imprisonment fueled by holding on to resentment, grief, and anger.

You decide. Me—I prefer to forgive.

Freedom

This is the F word most of us take for granted. When serious parenting duty calls, personal *freedom* is one of the first things to go. But it's critical that parents take time away from parenting. You may only be able to steal brief moments for yourself, especially early on, but that's better than nothing.

Go for a walk, read a good book (including this one!), visit a favorite museum, or see that hot new movie. Buy a café latte and savor every single drop. Shoot driveway hoops, practice meditation or deep breathing, write in a journal, or go prune the roses. Sit alone and enjoy the quiet in your house while the kids are at school—or blast loud rock music and dance as if you are possessed (watch your back).

Figure out what makes your life worth living each day and make it a priority.

Regain your sense of self, if only for a little while.

Friendship

It's one of the most powerful survival tools in your parenting arsenal. Nothing beats a good *friendship* for unconditional love and support. Friends have a way of reminding us of our talents and gifts when we've forgotten them. They accept our tears and flaws without judgment, and they offer a firm shoulder to lean on or a welcomed embrace. Real friends celebrate our successes and ease the sting of failure. When other support systems in our lives seem to be failing us, good friends rarely do.

Bless 'em all—never take good friends for granted.

Maintaining a Sense of Humor

By now, you have probably noticed that I like to poke fun at the absurdity of our daily demands, and a society that worships "expert" opinions (translation—lots of fancy degrees or celebrity) by using humor whenever appropriate (or not). My little hobby has kept me relatively sane.

I don't know what I would do without the comic genius of Robin Williams, Chris Rock, Bernie Mac, Ellen DeGeneres, Drew Carey and the whole cast of *Whose Line Is It Anyway?*—and Kathy Buckley. More about this funny lady in Chapter Ten.

Then there are my own unbelievable life adventures.

After parenting a child with cerebral palsy for more than a decade, here's another one of those valuable life lessons I've learned:

A good belly laugh has the power to heal what ails ya!

Some families may say that the daily demands of parenting a child with special needs leave them with little to laugh about, especially if their child has recently been diagnosed with special needs.

I understand such dark parenting moments well. I have survived more than my share of seemingly endless days with a crying, inconsolable infant. I have spent many sleepless nights at the intensive-care bedside of my critically ill toddler.

I remember how many days it took me to recover from all those depressing visits to humorless specialists who highlighted Eric's every flaw, without even looking at his face. I haven't forgotten the unending advocacy that's required to ensure that a child receives a good education. I attended more than my share of unnerving IEPs, and I know the heartache you feel as one more critical developmental milestone eludes your child.

I also believe that the intensity of parenting demands, including the grief over the death of my son, can often be positively soothed with a healthy dose of humor. Humor can be a critical survival tool on the uncertain special needs parenting journey.

Plus, I love to laugh! Laughing is good for your health. It offers you an important physical release for all those powerful emotions of grief, anger, and guilt (and the urge to kill) that so many parents choke back and swallow (think internal poison).

Parenting a child with special needs can be sobering, especially if that child is at risk of dying from those challenges. These children rarely respond to simple parenting solutions, and new challenges seem to be ready to pounce behind every parenting corner.

Having a good sense of humor about it all can help you survive most anything!

 DID YOU KNOW?

When I think of Paul Newman, I think of his ice blue eyes, great acting, and wonderful salad dressing. But did you know that Paul Newman has also made his dream of supporting camps for children with life-threatening illnesses come true? The Association of Hole in the Wall Camps (www.holeinthe wallcamps.org) offers children worldwide with tough health challenges, like HIV/AIDS, cancer, and sickle cell anemia, the opportunity to have a fun summer camp experience free of charge! The camp motto is "For kids with serious illnesses, laughter is the best medicine . . ." Check it out!

SURVIVING THE DEATH OF A CHILD

When I first decided to address the loss of a child in this book, I had no idea that I'd be using past tense to talk about my own son or writing about the death of the adult child of my friends Clare and Bill Leach.

I buried an incredible twelve-year-old preteen with a bright future. A year later, my friends lost their vibrant twenty-seven-year-old son, who also worked hard to rise above his special needs. The grief of their parenting loss is no less intense.

Parenting is for life. Your baby is always your baby, no matter what his age, no matter what package he comes in, no matter what his challenges. No parent should ever be asked to bury her child.

Both of our special needs success stories ended too soon.

Reflections on the Loss of My Son

Throughout the pages of *Breakthrough Parenting for Children with Special Needs*, I have shared many stories of my life with my son in the hope that your own parenting journey might prove less rocky. I've shared stories of celebration and moments that sting—but some sacred moments I'm keeping private.

The death of my son cuts deeply. I'm still figuring it out. I don't consider myself nearly as bold and wise on this topic as I do on lots of other stuff we've discussed.

As I reflect on my loss, it has only been two years since Eric died.

At times, it feels like yesterday.

But when I want desperately to hug Eric, hear his laugh, mess up his hair, and take him on another fun life adventure, it feels like an eternity has passed since he has been gone. The intense, unexpected longing and emptiness that I still feel unnerves me.

The loss of a child shakes you deep down in your bones, no matter what else life has thrown at you—no matter what a big-shot advocate and survivor you think you've become. I'm just beginning to understand why parents never really get over the death their child.

When you have a child with special needs, so much of your time, emotion, and energy is spent protecting and defending that child that when death comes knocking rudely in the middle of the night and steals him away, the insult is especially cruel. The reality leaves you wailing at the moon—and rightly so.

Two years later, after my son's death, I don't wail at the moon every day. My moaning is gentler, more internalized, not always for the world to hear. I'm quieter, more accepting of my grief. I will always deeply mourn the loss of my son, and too many days, I still fall to my knees. There's comfort there.

When I do start strutting around like my life is back on track, the grief gods like to swoop down and knock me on the side of my head. "You aren't *really* in control of your life." they mock loudly.

And they're right. When your child dies, one of the first things you learn is how little control any of us really has over the big moments in life that blindside us.

In the words of my friend Al Swain, most of the stuff we get all bent out of shape about in life ain't that big a deal. Death is a big deal. Death jerks around the predictable world order of things.

Many parents of children with special needs know somewhere deep in their hearts that an early death is possible. Still, we chose to live life as if Eric would outlive us all. I believed that this gentle giant just might be the one to cheat the ugly, life-expectancy odds—even as we worried about who would possibly give Eric the quality of life he was used to if we were to die first—a concern of many families.

I would have done anything for my son. The reality that I could not protect him from an early death has been a struggle for me. Yet I don't feel guilty; I just feel incredibly human. Many parents face survivor's guilt (adding insult to injury). They torture themselves with all those *What ifs? Why didn't I?* and *If onlys*. I prefer not to risk climbing that slippery precipice.

The snotty little guilt gremlins will eat you up alive, if you let 'em. So I'm working hard to preserve and honor Eric's memory and life lessons instead, trying to make sense of the senseless by helping other children avoid some of the same societal land mines my son faced. I plan to continue to work to create a greater awareness and understanding of children with special needs and advocate for necessary change.

The work is endless.

The payoff for living and loving your child well is having no regrets. But the tears still come far too easily, at unexpected times and in weird places, and I've learned to honor that, too. I will never be the same person I was before Eric's death, but I don't want to be. I'm the ultimate survivor, but the price I have been asked to pay is huge.

My advice to parents facing loss is to live fully, love fully, grieve fully, be gentle with yourself, and then move on—but never ever forget your child. Use your wounds to make the world a better place. In your humanitarian actions (find a need and fill it!), lies real healing. And a reason to go on living.

. . . Wherever you are, Eric Richard Winter, I hope you are as proud of me as I am of you. You are finally soaring free, and even in my deepest sorrow, that realization brings me peace—and makes me smile! I love you with all my heart and soul, RicStar—forever and always, infinity!

Facing the Death of an Older Child

Bill and Clare Leach live in Aspen, Colorado, and own a successful art gallery. Amid the celebrity glitz that often defines the popular ski resort, the couple had worked hard to build a close family unit with their two adult sons. Clare Leach had raised Brian and Tim as her own after their parents divorced when they were children.

"I never intended to marry a man with two children," Clare says. "But I fell deeply in love with this man when I was thirty. The boys were so terrific and I wanted to be part of that family." Clare admits that everyone had to make adjustments to make the new stepfamily work. "It took about three years to really feel like we were a family, but we made it and the four of us functioned as a close family unit for many years," she says. "I wouldn't trade one moment of being part of this family even with all the adjustments that came with being a stepparent. I feel incredibly lucky."

Clare has been a licensed professional counselor (LPC) for thirty years. She specializes in addressing the needs of couples, adolescents, adult children of alcoholics, and those facing issues around divorce, marriage, depression, and loss. She never dreamed she'd be grieving the loss of her youngest stepson.

Tim Leach was born with a partially open palate and tongue misplacement and didn't speak clearly until he was age three. He was teased at school. Tim received speech therapy services until the fifth grade and tutoring support for his reading challenges. He worked hard to rise above special needs. As an adult, he still slurred his words when he was tired.

Tim graduated from the University of Virginia in 1998 with a degree in psychology, then received a master's degree in social work (MSW) from Virginia Commonwealth. In 2002, he fulfilled his childhood dream of joining his stepmom's thriving Aspen practice.

An expert skier, Tim was used to the challenges of the slopes of the nearby Snowmass Ski Area, where he had skied many times. But on March 18, 2004, after enjoying an afternoon of skiing with good friends, Tim turned a corner sharply in icy conditions and hit a tree. The helmet he always wore wasn't enough to save his life.

For two days, Tim Leach clung to life with a closed head injury, before his parents honored his wish to donate his organs. The fact that no physical signs of injury were obvious on his body made this decision especially tough. Tim Leach never regained consciousness, but his gifts that day saved the lives of at least four people. He was just twenty-seven years old when he died—a beloved son, husband, brother, friend, and therapist. The loss cuts deep.

Like many others, the Leach family is now working hard to make sense of what seems like an unimaginable tragedy—and every parent's nightmare.

As a skilled professional counselor and parent who now understands tough loss firsthand, Clare Leach shares her professional wisdom with families who are trying to resolve grief issues surrounding special needs parenting.

We have both found healing by honoring our children in this way.

 ## CLARE LEACH'S TIPS

Grieving and Loss

In the depths of your great pain and loss, it's tough to believe any "tips" could possibly help ease your grief; but believe me, these can.

- *Don't suppress your pain.* Grieve with all your heart and soul.   *(continued on next page)*

(continued from previous page)

- *Don't let anyone tell you how long or how to grieve.* Don't put time limits on yourself. "A child is an eternal heart connection. The best hope is that raw pain will be replaced with a sense of peace and integration of the loss. You will never be the same. Bitterness will not bring a child back."

- *Celebrate your child's life.* "Talk about your child often, and do something for other children who need special help in whatever way you find appropriate." A thank-you letter on the first anniversary of Tim's death from the woman who had received his kidney helped the Leach family survive the first-year anniversary of Tim's death. I have found that leaving beautiful flowers at Eric's grave site each week is helping me heal.

- *Stop asking why.* Even if there are answers, they may not help heal your pain.

- *Don't take insensitive comments about your loss personally.* "Our culture is not comfortable talking about grief. Friends who haven't lost a child may want to comfort you but may not know how. Understand that, like us, they are doing the best they know how." Tell people what you need from them, but don't be disappointed if they can't or won't provide it. And don't be surprised to find that your circle of friends changes.

- *Attend a grief and loss support group.* "This is especially helpful in the early months following the death of a child. You may learn how to help each other grieve and better understand your own individual grieving styles."

- *Find healing and comfort in honoring memories.* "We would never trade one moment of having had Tim in our lives, even as we face the intensity of the loss." I echo that heartfelt mother's sentiment.

- *Seek professional help and access good resources.* "If you are struggling with loss, get help." You are dealing with the greatest loss anyone can ever face and few survive it alone.

Some of Clare's favorite books are *On Grief and Dying*, by Elisabeth Kübler-Ross; *All Is Not Lost*, by C. Leslie Charles; *Words of Comfort*, by Helen Exley. (Other great resources on grief and loss may be found on page 196.)

Clare Leach offers additional advice for couples facing a variety of grief issues surrounding special needs parenting:

- *Make every day count.* "Never assume you will outlive your child." Understand that each of you will grieve loss in different ways. That's OK.

- *Take care of yourself and of each other.* "Spend quality time alone to regroup. Talk about your loss and be fully present for each other. After a death, you may find you want more or less physical contact." Do what works for you.

- *Do not run from each other.* "Have date nights and get out of the house, even when you don't feel like it." Avoid deadly isolation.

- *Do not blame or avoid your spouse.* "Listen carefully and do not judge each other's pain or grieving styles." Support each other instead.

- *Learn about the stages of grief.* "Like shock and denial, what if? and if only, depression, anger, and resolution. You may experience all these stages and maybe more than once— even if your child is still living." Understanding these stages can help make them less frightening.

- *Finally, find people who are ahead of you in the grief–special needs survival process.* Allow them to serve as mentors (if

(continued on next page)

(continued from previous page)

they are willing and able). "Such support is priceless, because it gives us hope that we can and will survive— breath by breath, whatever loss we face."

SPECIAL TIPS

Here are a few ideas to help you nurture yourself daily. They'll help keep you focused on the good things still in your life that you can be grateful for.

- *Celebrate the smallest miracles every day of your child's life.* We can get so caught up in the focus on what's "wrong" with our kids that it's easy to overlook the good stuff they do. Acknowledging your child's accomplishments, however small, can help keep your challenges in perspective and help remind you of your child's value. That's good for your parenting heart and soul, and your perspective.

- *Keep a gratitude–self-care journal.* Make at least three entries about the day's blessings before going to bed each night. End the day focused on gratitude. This powerful shift in thinking is a great way to finish the day, no matter how tough it's been. You can *still* turn it around.

- *Don't go to bed mad.* Talk things out and resolve your differences instead. It's much better for your health, your marriage, and the well-being of your family. Addressing your emotional needs is a critical part of self-care. Take time for it.

Special Resources

Here are some more great resources that will provide helpful information.

Blindness, Visual Impairment, Multiple Sclerosis, and Other Disabilities

- American Federation for the Blind (AFB): www.afb.org.
- Prevent Blindness America—Children: http://www.prevent blindness.org/children/.
- United States Association of Blind Athletes (USABA): www.usaba.org.
- National Association for Parents of Children with Visual Impairments (NAPVI): http://www.spedex.com/napvi/.
- Al Swain: Capital Area Center for Independent Living: aswain@cacil.org.
- National Council on Independent Living (NCL): www.ncil.org: link to statewide directory of independent living centers.
- National Multiple Sclerosis Society (NMSS): http://www.nmss.org, or call the twenty-four-hour information line at 1-800-FIGHT MS (1-800-344-4867).
- National Multiple Sclerosis Society, Arney Rosenblat, public affairs director: Arney.Rosenblat@nmss.org.
- National Pediatric MS Center: http://www.pediatricmscen ter.org/.
- Young Persons with MS: A Network for Families with a Child or Teen with MS: www.childhoodms@nmss.org (1-866-543-7967).
- The American Sickle Cell Anemia Association: http://www.ascaa.org.
- St. Jude Children's Research Hospitals: www.stjude.org.
- Juvenile Diabetes Research Foundation International (JDRF): www.jdf.org.

- Obsessive-Compulsive Foundation (OCD): www. ocfoundation.org.
- Tourette Syndrome Association, Inc.: http://tsa-usa.org.

Grief and Loss (also see page 193)

- *Understanding Your Grief, The Understanding Your Grief Journal, Healing a Parent's Grieving Heart: 100 Practical Ideas After Your Child Dies,* and *Creating Meaningful Funeral Experiences: A Guide for Caregivers,* by Alan D. Wolfelt, Ph.D. / The Center for Loss and Life Transition: www.centerforloss.com.
- *Helping People with Developmental Disabilities Mourn: Practical Rituals for Caregivers,* by Alan D. Wolfelt, Ph.D., and Marck A. Markell, Ph.D.
- The Compassionate Friends: http://www.compassionate friends.org.
- The Living with Loss Foundation: http://LivingwithLoss.org.
- Bereavement Magazine: http://www.bereavementmag.com.

Health and Family

- *Eight Weeks to Optimum Health,* by Andrew Weil, M.D.
- *Don't Sweat the Small Stuff with Your Family: Simple Ways to Keep Daily Responsibilities and Household Chaos from Taking Over Your Life,* by Richard Carlson, Ph.D.

Organ Donation

- Medline Plus: U.S. National Library and the National Institute of Health (NIH): www.nlm.nih.gov/medlineplus/ organdonation.html.

Respite and Other Assistance

- ARCH National Resource Center for Respite and Crisis Care Services: www.archrespite.org: offers the National Respite Locator Service.

- Family Caregiver Alliance (FCA): www.caregiver.org.
- Caregiver.com: *Today's Caregiver* magazine.
- Centers for Medicare and Medicaid Services: www.cms.hhs.gov.

Speech and Language Disorders

- Cleft Palate Foundation (CLF): http://www.cleftline.org.
- Kid Source Online: NICHCY information about speech and language disorders: http://www.kidsource.com/ NICHCY/speech.html.
- Apraxia Kids: http://www.apraxia-kids.org.
- CHERAB: http://www.cherab.org/index.html.
- National Stuttering Association (NSA): http://www. nsastutter.org.

Special Note

There's a good reason why flight attendants tell you to put the oxygen mask on yourself first in case of an emergency, *before* offering it to a child. It's nearly impossible to expend the energy required to help a child if you can't breathe yourself or if you aren't even alive! When it comes to special needs parenting, it's not only OK to take care of yourself—it's critical! Prioritize!

It's time to address one of the most important special needs parenting topics in this book: meeting the needs of siblings (about time!). Let's find out just what some of these kids really think about life with special needs. Siblings are my heroes. They deserve to be heard, too.

9

MEETING THE NEEDS OF SIBLINGS

It is not difficult to fill the hand of a child.

—Chinese Proverb

In the special needs parenting adventure, siblings are real-life heroes.

Through no fault of their own, they are asked to endure the reality of living with a brother or sister with special needs and all that it entails.

The reality can easily interfere with getting their own needs met. Unlike many of their peers, these siblings are expected to take on the kind of mature roles that may help them grow into confident, self-sufficient, and sensitive young adults—as they are robbed of a more carefree youth.

This chapter explores the important role of siblings in families with special needs—past and present. We're shining a light on the needs of siblings to help parents better recognize and understand the importance of meeting those needs. You will learn about the Sibling Support Project of the Arc of the United States and Sibshops, and you'll benefit from the heartfelt words of wisdom from just a few siblings who have made their families proud.

We begin with the story of a family whose special needs parenting role recently ended, yet their positive example of meeting sibling needs is worth sharing. This family worked hard to meet the needs of four children, no matter what special needs demanded of them each day. Now they are savoring the fruits of their twenty-five-year parenting commitment.

We can all learn from their success.

A SUCCESS STORY

After the death of a child with special needs—when the parenting and grief dust has settled a bit—some families are able to look back with greater clarity and objectivity about the importance of their past parenting choices.

The Schneider family must have done something right—they have raised three well-adjusted siblings, who appear to have become even closer since the death of their twenty-five-year-old sister with special needs in August 2002.

Jessica Emery Schneider was diagnosed with an intellectual disability, an anxiety disorder, and a seizure disorder. The family spent years trying a variety of drugs and medical treatments to help control the seizures that first began at age fifteen. But nothing had worked. Jessica drowned at her family's cottage after having another of her increasingly frequent seizures.

John Schneider, fifty-six, and Sharon Emery, fifty-two, are Jessica's parents and have been married for thirty years. John is an award-winning daily columnist and feature writer for the *Lansing State Journal* (Gannett) in Michigan's capital city.

He's also the author of *Waiting for Home. The Richard Prangley Story*, which tells the story of a man unjustly institutionalized in 1955 and abandoned by his parents. (Since his release in 1971, Richard Prangley has worked full time, owns his own home, and has become an effective disability advocate.)

Sharon Emery is an editor-reporter for the Lansing Bureau of Booth Newspapers. She has a master's degree from the Graduate School of Journalism at Columbia University in New York City, has completed doctoral work in mass media, and has taught journalism courses at Michigan State University. In 2002, she completed a fellowship in ethics and special needs at the University of Michigan.

That's impressive stuff—but Sharon Emery says that first and foremost she's a wife and mother. "My first reaction to Jessica's death was 'Why was this job taken away from me?' I was doing a great job at being her mom," Sharon says. "I was really angry about this loss for several months after she died."

Sharon and John have always prioritized marriage and family. The result of their solid family focus is evident in the accomplishments of their three remaining children, who exhibit close and loving sibling relationships. "We always felt we were in this special needs parenting thing together," John says of the couple's efforts to meet their parenting challenges.

Their thoughtful parenting decisions seem to have stuck—all of their children are now confidently pursuing their individual life dreams.

Oldest son Justin, age twenty-five, is a graduate of Michigan State University and a feature writer for a Michigan newspaper. He's following in his parent's well-established professional footsteps.

Benjamin, twenty-one, is completing his art degree at the University of Michigan and studying French abroad at the popular University Aix-Marseilles III in Provence. Benjamin is a talented and award-winning artist; his work has been exhibited in Michigan art galleries, and he has already sold several pieces.

At age eighteen, Caitlin is the baby of the bunch, preparing to graduate from high school and attend the University of Michigan. She admits it wasn't easy living in a family with special needs. "But I didn't know anything else," she says. "My sister was older than me, so she was always a part of my life."

As Caitlin grew up, she faced responsibilities that most of the kids her age don't, such as being required to come home after school each day to be with Jessica while her parents were at work. Her sister's unpredictable tantrums and behavior challenges, especially in public, were often tough to deal with. "I knew that my parents needed to focus more attention on Jessica than me when we were together because of the nature of her disabilities," Caitlin says.

She appreciates the fact that her parents worked hard to address and resolve Jessica's challenges but also made time for her. "One person was at the soccer game and one person was with Jess," Caitlin says. "They were very aware of giving us all equal time. I felt I was just as important as my sister, who at times was screaming a lot louder."

"We never gave up on Jessica, or on helping her modify her behavior," John says, "because we knew she had to function in the world. We made sure Jessica was included," he continues. "Even though it was risky business to go out in public with her at times, we always treated her with respect."

"We were taught to be proud of our sister," Caitlin adds. "My parents didn't just talk to us about treating my sister like a valued family member, they modeled it for us."

Before Jessica died, Caitlin and her brother Justin had made future plans to take care of their sister. "We didn't want her to go to a home," Caitlin says. "We knew there was an innate sacrifice in taking on this responsibility, but we wanted to do it," she says. "So we planned to finish college, get our careers started, and then move back home to take care of Jess."

The personal freedom and quieter household that the family has gained since Jessica's death pales in comparison to the magnitude of their loss. "What I miss most about Jessica is how I got to act whenever I was with her—the silliness we shared when we were together," Caitlin explains. "Because of Jessica's needs, I had to grow up really fast, but Jess was the one person I could be most idiotic with," she says. "I'm still a kid at heart."

"I miss her guilelessness," John adds of his fishing buddy. "Jessica's emotions were always on her sleeve. If she was ticked off at you, you knew it. You always knew where you stood with Jess." John says that humor has helped his family cope with their challenges over the years and remain close.

Caitlin's experience with special needs has affected her in ways that even surprised her parents. "When it was time to plan for college, I was a bit bitter about my sister's death," Caitlin admits. "I no longer had my sister's special needs as an excuse not to do the best I could do in life."

It's an unexpected twist to this honest sibling dialogue.

"My sister also taught me a lot about patience," she adds. "Now I wish I had been more patient and more attentive to her while she was still here." But Caitlin says it's important for siblings to be able to complain, too, something she feels free to do with her brothers and her parents.

The family's closeness and faith have helped them survive special needs and the loss of one of their own. The siblings continue to draw strength from one another. "The best part today is seeing that the kids are all friends," John says proudly. "I believe that our whole family will be together again one day."

"Our family did the best we could with special needs, and I think that was pretty good," Caitlin Schneider says. "My sister was happy."

The Schneiders' story is a powerful reminder to families of the importance of balancing special needs and sibling needs. Because experience is a pretty darn good teacher, here's another example of a loving family that's working hard every day to meet the needs of their two younger children.

Meeting the Needs of Younger Siblings

As the youngest sibling in her family, Caitlin Schneider had always lived with her sister's special needs. The roles are reversed in the Frayer family, but some of the sibling challenges aren't all that much different.

When it comes to her role as a big sister in a family with special needs, Megan Frayer has lots to say—and she's not afraid to say it. Megan is a bright, charming, twelve-year-old seventh grader who's had her life mapped out since age six. Her plans include attending Michigan State University and writing for *Wildlife Conservation* magazine. "So I can travel all over the world and write about conservation!" the animal lover says.

Megan is glad to be the oldest sibling in her family. "I got really lucky," she says. "It's fun having a little sister because they look up to you."

Her little sister, Katie, was born with a rare form of *arthrogryposis* called *arthrogryposis multiplex congenita* (AMC), which causes tight muscles and joints, results in muscle weakness, and limits her range of motion.

Katie is an enchanting eight-year-old second grader, who loves school, playing tag in her power wheelchair, taking trips to Disney World, and eating tons of Parmesan cheese—plain!

Katie has scoliosis and is at risk for early arthritis, but her disability is not considered progressive. She's excited about an upcoming swimming competition for Special Olympics and wants to become a doctor, because "I already understand what kids go through."

As a young child, Megan remembers going to many of Katie's daily therapies, something that began early in Katie's life. "There is a whole lot of waiting in doctors' offices," she admits of the sibling's family role, one that can prove quite stressful. "I used to think that if anything every happened to Katie, I would be very mad at the doctors," Megan recalls. These siblings are close.

"It was great when Megan was finally in school all day," her mom, Beth Frayer, admits. "Then she didn't have to go with us all the time to Katie's appointments."

"The attention issue is what people often put the focus on with siblings, but we found that the uncertainty around Katie's condition early on really impacted Megan," says their father, Dave Frayer. "Megan was the only child for four-and-one-half years."

The change in her only-child status resulted in some acting out, Dave says, a combination of sibling jealousy and concern about her sister's well-being. "We finally realized that Megan's behavior was almost always connected to a major event in Katie's life, like a major medical appointment."

"I used to get confused because of Katie's disability and because there wasn't enough time for me," Megan says. She remembers some of the times when she got really mad and yelled. She describes it as "having a meltdown" and says it doesn't happen much now that she's older. "Sometimes I still vent my anger at my mom," she says, "because my mom really listens.

"But don't vent your anger on your sibling, especially if they are younger," Megan advises other siblings. "If I get mad, and Katie cries, then I get in trouble. It doesn't always work out well."

Even though Megan admits she's not always thrilled with the challenges special needs demands of her, she would do anything for her little sister and worries about her. "Sometimes I worry that Katie won't be able to be what she wants to be when she grows up because of her disability—and that would stink."

Megan's role has changed as she has gotten older and become involved in more of her own activities. She's taking tai kwon do, participates in Girl Scouts, volunteers at a summer camp for special needs, and can now be left home alone for periods of time. "We let Megan know that she's not Katie's mom. She has a sisterly duty," Beth says. "But it's not a caretaker role."

The family keeps an open line of communication with both girls and prioritizes one-on-one time for each. "We have also explained to Megan that therapy is not one-on-one time with Katie," Beth explains. "It's something we have to do to meet Katie's physical needs."

The siblings are both grateful to have a loving family that travels together often, attends church regularly, and places a high priority on family time. "Time is going so fast," Beth Frayer says. "We just want to enjoy every moment."

When asked the best part about being a member of her family, Katie quickly looks at Megan and says, "My big sister." Megan flashes back a huge grin. When Katie drops something on the floor, Megan picks it up and gently hands it to her younger sibling, while answering another question about her own role in this special family—all without missing a beat.

Megan Frayer clearly enjoys her role as Katie's big sister, special needs challenges and all.

THE FRAYER FAMILY'S TIPS
Siblings and Parents

Beth, Dave, Megan, and Katie Frayer share what they have learned about how to be proactive in addressing the challenges that can arise with siblings of kids with special needs (people-first language).

- *Don't deny your child's feelings.* Talk about them instead. "It's very easy to misread confusion, nervousness, or anxiety for jealousy, especially in younger children," Dave Frayer says. This couple finally realized that Megan's acting out as a young child was often linked to something big going on in Katie's life, like a major medical event.

- *Find ways to include siblings in various therapies.* Siblings must often go to therapies or other appointments with their brother or sisters, especially when they are young, so try to include them. "For example, if games are being played, include them in the activity, too," Beth suggests.

- *Go out in public as a family.* "It's important that people see Katie around town, at church, and at school," Beth says. "It helps people understand that disability is a part of life. Katie has a right to go wherever we go." Her mom is not afraid to address accessibility issues. "I tell people they need to make room for Katie because she's coming through."

Megan offers these words of wisdom:

- *Remember that you are not the only one with a brother or sister with special needs.* "Sometimes Katie's annoying, but I don't know what I would do if anything ever happened

(continued on next page)

(continued from previous page)

to her," Megan Frayer says. "There's always someone who has it worse than you."

- *Stand up for your sibling with special needs.* "I shouldn't have to be Katie's protector, but if someone is picking on her, I will stand up for her."

- *Be considerate of the sibling without disabilities, too.* "Don't focus solely on the child with special needs. So many people ask how Katie's doing when I'm standing in front of them." Megan says. "Ask how I'm doing, too."

- *Help other kids better understand people with special needs.* "I feel sorry for people who don't get differences and are mean to people with special needs, because they are missing out. People with disabilities aren't that much different from anyone else."

- *Don't always assume that problems with school or behavior challenges are the result of a sibling's special needs.* "Your child may have had a fight with a friend, or maybe somebody was mean to them at school," Megan says. "Not everything that happens in a sibling's life is caused by special needs."

- *Spend one-on-one time with siblings.* "Bedtime is my special time with my mom," Megan says. "We aren't just talking about Katie's needs."

- *Be honest with your child about her sibling's needs.* Megan says her parents don't try to hide the truth from her. "If something happened to Katie and they didn't tell me," she says, "I would feel much worse."

- *Have positive role models outside the family.* Megan loves Dr. Jane Goodall.

- *Focus on the positives of your role.* "I get to go to the front of the line at Disney World!" Megan points out.

DID YOU KNOW?

Virginia Simson Nelson, M.D., MPH, of the University of Michigan's Department of Physical Medicine and Rehabilitation and C. S. Mott Children's Hospital in Ann Arbor is one of the few experts on *arthrogryposis* in the world and Katie Frayer's rehab physician. "Arthrogryposis is a wastebasket term that means stuck joints," Dr. Nelson explains. "Most children are diagnosed at birth because they are born with multiple contractures: a number of joints that don't move the way they are supposed to. It may be part of a syndrome or genetic condition or just an isolated thing. It is a diagnosis of exclusion."

For more information about this rare disability, contact Dr. Virginia Simson Nelson at (734) 936-7200 or by e-mail: pedsrehab@umich.edu.

Avoiding the Perfect-Sibling Syndrome

With the support of a loving family, the sibling experience can result in rich life lessons that serve our children well. The family unit can survive, even thrive, under the most challenging special needs conditions.

But as the words of the siblings in this chapter show, it's not always easy being the brother or sister of a child with special needs. Research indicates that siblings of children with special needs are at greater risk for depression, tend to be overachievers to make up for the shortcomings of their brothers or sisters, and may bury their needs to avoid adding conflict to already stressed-out families. Many say they try to be *good kids* and not make waves, making it especially important that parents tune in. I call it the *perfect-sibling syndrome*— an impossible goal for any child to attain.

As with the other siblings we've met in this chapter, my good buddy Nick Saur is fortunate to be part of a loving, supportive family—which can help neutralize the tough quest for sibling perfection. We met Nick's family in Chapters Five and Six. His older sibling, Dan, has cerebral palsy and uses a wheelchair.

Nick is a thirteen-year-old seventh grader, who once lived with his family in Budapest, Hungary, so his older brother could receive conductive education. When it comes to Dan's needs, Nick is used to going with the family flow.

Family means everything to Nick. They spend lots of time together, including at the Northern Michigan cottage they built themselves. "My parents spent a lot of time focusing just on me, and that's really important to me," Nick says. Such attention is invaluable to siblings facing the fallout of special needs.

At home, Nick loves spending one-on-one time with his dad and fixing up an old sailboat in their garage. "I get to do it with my dad guiding me," he says. "It's our time together, when we can get away from everything else."

Nick accepts the reality that his future will probably include taking some responsibility for his older brother. "If Dan can't drive or find someone to take care of him, I will probably take care of him a lot of the time," he says. "But I'd like to be a harbormaster."

Nick offers some advice to other siblings. "Always think positive and let your needs be known," he says. "If you need help with anything, ask!"

Here's part of a letter Nick recently wrote about his older sibling, Dan:

Having a brother with cerebral palsy has its ups and downs. I get to park closer to the grocery store on rainy days and take rides on the back of Dan's wheelchair. But he can't do all the things I like to do easily, like play basketball with my friends, or stay up all night and play flashlight tag and other outdoor stuff. Sometimes it saddens me when I think of Dan sitting in his wheelchair inside on a beautiful summer day when I am having an excellent time outdoors. My friends ask why I always come home and check in rather than stay out later, but I want to know that my brother is okay.

When I think of something that I am very thankful for, one is my ability to walk and communicate easily with others. Dan doesn't have those kinds of abilities, so I would like to trade lives with him just once, so Dan could see what it is like walking, talking, and being freed from the wheelchair that has held him hostage for eighteen years.

Every once and a while I wonder what it would be like if Dan could walk and talk. But my brother doesn't embarrass me because I know if other people got to know him, they would know how cool he really is. But I wish that I could take our dog Moose out for a walk and not have to push Dan in a jogger. I wish he could just walk alongside me, and play sports with me.

Dan is by far the toughest person I know and he's smart about computers! I love to make him laugh, because when he is happy, I'm also happy—when he's mad, he runs over my foot! Dan has taught me not to go with the crowd, and made me a more mature kid. I've learned to try to be as kind to everyone as I am to Dan.

I love my brother so much and I wouldn't trade him for anything in the world. I am so proud of him and I know that because of our family, Dan will be one of the fortunate ones with special needs to succeed in life.

The insightful words of all the siblings shared in this chapter remind me why I think they're something special—and I'm not alone in my admiration.

THE SIBLING SUPPORT PROJECT AND SIBSHOPS ROCK

When it comes to recognizing the important needs of siblings in special needs families, perhaps no other professional is more committed to the cause than Don Meyer.

Meyer is director of the Sibling Support Project of the Arc of the United States (http://www.thearc.org/siblingsupport), a national organization dedicated to the lifelong concerns of the more than 6.5 million brothers and sisters of siblings with health, developmental, and mental health concerns.

The project is best known for Sibshops, an award-winning program that offers siblings in families with special needs a rare and valuable opportunity to interact with their peers in group meetings held in recreational settings and led by trained personnel. "Sibshops offer peer support and education programs for siblings of school-aged kids with special needs," Meyer explains.

"Sibshops is an opportunity for siblings to meet peers, have fun, and talk about the good and not-so-good parts of being a sib, and everything in between," Meyer adds. "Kids get to play goofy games, learn how other siblings handle their situations, eat junky kid food, learn about program services for siblings, and then have some more fun."

There are now 160 Sibshops in ten countries. "We offer peer support and information within a recreational context," Meyer says. "We believe that just as parents get something out of connecting with their peers, so do brothers and sisters."

Meyer explains that sibling experiences parallel parent experiences. "Plus, siblings have some experiences that are uniquely theirs, such as embarrassment, guilt, pressure to be the 'good kid,' peer issues, concerns about the future, even resentment," he says.

"Our argument is that just about anything you can say about what it's like being the parent of a child with special needs, you can put 'ditto' marks underneath for siblings. A sibling relationship is the working definition of ambivalence," Meyer says. "It's about hugging and slugging. That's increased when a brother or sister has a disability. The highs are higher and the lows are lower."

He points out that most brothers and sisters will be in the lives of a family member with special needs longer than anyone else, making that relationship especially critical. "Brothers and sisters will have far greater impact on the social development of a child with special needs than any classmate in an inclusive classroom," Meyer stresses.

He further explains that the needs and concerns of siblings evolve and change throughout the life of the family. Meyer shares just a few of the benefits of a sibling's valuable role, while cautioning against taking a Pollyanna stance on the subject. "These are hard-won sibling opportunities," he says.

- They often develop maturity, patience, diplomacy, and tolerance at a younger age than their peers. "They learn that it's OK to be different."

- They often have insight into the human condition and an expanded understanding of life.

- They often grow up to be powerful advocates, even at a young age.

- They are often more certain of their own future and vocational goals than their peers and often gravitate toward helping professions (an added benefit to society).

- They are often fiercely loyal. "They may fight within the family, but the outside world wouldn't want to mess with their brothers and sisters."

DON MEYER'S TIPS

Siblings

As director of the Sibling Support Project, Don Meyer offers these helpful tips:

- *Brothers and sisters need age-appropriate information from a variety of sources.* "Siblings have a lifelong and ever-changing need for information. Children in preschool will have a need for different information than siblings in high school, college, or adulthood. Needs and responsibilities will change. Parents should make this an open topic for discussion, something you can always talk

(continued on next page)

(continued from previous page)

about." A note to professionals: Meyer says the challenge they face is to be increasingly family friendly and proactive in reaching out to siblings in special needs families. "I continually have to remind others that brothers and sisters are part of these families," Meyer says. "If you are interested in serving families and offering family-centered care, then you need to make yourself available to brothers and sisters, too."

- *Siblings in special needs families need opportunities to meet other siblings.* Meyer says they can meet through Sibshops, or more informally doing things like camping with other families, meeting on listservs, or reading a book, like Meyer's most recent project, *The Sibling Slam: What It's Really Like to Have a Brother or Sister with Special Needs.* "I wanted to give young readers a chance to meet other sibs in a book that tells it like it is."

- *We all have an obligation to find out more about life as a sibling in a family with special needs.* Meyer moderates panels, conducts workshops, and speaks at conferences. He suggests that others do things like read books, including *Riding the Bus with My Sister: A True Life Journey*, by Rachel Simon, which Meyer calls "a wonderfully rich read." He also recommends *Special Siblings: Growing up with Someone with a Disability*, by Mary McHugh and *The Ride Together: A Brother and Sister's Memoir of Autism in the Family*, by Paul Karasik and Judy Karasik. (See more of Meyer's own book titles under resources on pages 218–219.)

- *Parents should try to reassure their children by making plans for the future and then sharing those plans with siblings.* "Don't think you're doing them a favor by playing those cards close to the chest," Meyer says. "These siblings tend to be incredibly generous and are good at putting others' needs first. They need to be encouraged to take care of themselves."

- *Remember that the single strongest factor in determining how well siblings handle their role is the parent's interpretation of their own special needs parenting situation.* "If a parent sees it as a series of challenges to meet with as much grace and humor as they can muster, then at the end of the day, they have every reason to believe their kids will perceive it that way, too," Meyer says. "That doesn't mean it won't be a bumpy ride at times."

 DID YOU KNOW?

According to Don Meyer, director of the Sibling Support Project of the Arc of the United States, the organization offers the Internet's only listservs for and about brothers and sisters of people with special health, developmental, and emotional needs. By accessing SibKids (for younger siblings), and SibNet (for adult siblings), siblings of all ages can connect worldwide to share their experiences growing up in a family with special needs. SibGroup gives adults who run sibling programs worldwide the opportunity to connect with their colleagues free of charge. For more information, and for a listing of Sibshops worldwide, visit: www.thearc.org/siblingsupport. Check it out!

Reflecting on Jenna's Important Sibling Role

Of all the emotional heartbreak that parents of children with special needs are asked to face, perhaps none stings more than knowing a sibling's life could have been easier.

Through no fault of their own, siblings are asked to cope with the loss of a simpler and more normal family life. They often do without regular family outings and vacations. They may be afraid their siblings will embarrass them in front of their peers or at the mall. They often wonder how special needs in the family will affect their own social life, future plans, and responsibilities—concerns that may go unanswered by their parents.

My baby girl was six years old, the first grandchild in the family, and the center of our world. She was a bright, beautiful, and engaging child, everything a new parent hopes for. In the perfect-baby game, she was the grand prize. Then her brother came along and blew everyone's world apart and redefined perfection. Our lives were never the same—we were given new parenting gifts.

Today we are trying to re-create some moments we lost years ago with our firstborn, like spending uninterrupted time with this independent and talented young woman. Our dinners together are now without distraction and are more leisurely. Planned social outings and frequent travel go much smoother.

Now when we talk, I hear every single word Jenna has to say. Still, something is missing, not unlike in the Schneider family. A part of me knows we're trying hard to make up to Jenna for lost parenting time—hers. The goal is OK, but bittersweet—because underneath all the well-intentioned effort, we all still miss Eric deeply. Our wounds are much too fresh . . .

From the beginning of our special needs parenting adventure, we promised Jenna that her brother's special needs wouldn't short-change her life dreams. It wasn't always easy keeping that promise—but we tried hard.

We were determined that both children inherit rich family memories, which included unconditional love, an understanding of diversity, and good problem-solving skills, rather than a legacy of guilt, resentment, and emotional injury. We put our parenting plans into action—and prayed for the best.

Jenna enjoyed dance classes, summer camp, horseback riding, choir and church events, drama, yearbook, competitive cheerleading, and travels abroad as a student ambassador to Europe and Australia. We traveled many times to Northern Michigan, went to the movies, and ate dinner as a family often.

To the outside world, my daughter didn't appear to have gotten the short end of the parenting stick. At times, I felt differently. So did she. I remember the many times I returned home late after spending hours in intensive-care units, desperate for sleep. But my daughter needed to express her sense of loss and anger over having a brother with special needs, who always took top priority. These emotional exchanges ended with hugs, laughter, and tears.

Seeing her innocent, tear-stained faced was jolting. It still is.

I remember how often we were required to tag team to ensure that one parent would be present at all Jenna's events. At times, our best intentions were shot down by emergency hospitalizations and sudden illnesses. We didn't always reach our lofty parenting goals—others were cut short.

But our daughter knew we loved her and that her future was her own. We told her that we expected her to love and respect her brother, but she was not his caretaker. We hugged her as tightly and as often as she would allow and always welcomed her friends into our home, where they often happily hung out.

When she graduated from high school, Jenna moved across the country to take on the demanding curriculum at a fine arts college in Southern California. I was neither confident nor mature enough to do that at her age.

Today Jenna exhibits high self-esteem, a wisdom beyond her years, a great heart, and true concern for those who struggle. She is beautiful inside and out and a role model for all siblings. She was a wonderful big sister to Eric.

I admit that I'm relieved that Jenna no longer has to worry about future responsibility for her brother, but the why still cuts deeply. I wonder if she will ever fully understand how hard we worked in light of special needs to ensure that she and Eric would both grow into healthy, productive adulthood.

I don't think I'll ever find the words to tell this child exactly what she means to me and how I wish her childhood could have been easier. My heart aches when I think of the leisurely mother-daughter moments we missed because of my parenting demands.

At times, I've felt slightly cheated, too.

But neither of us would choose life without her much-loved sibling.

Jenna's Reflections on Life with Her Brother

With the benefit of time, Jenna looks back at life with her little brother.

> In her song "Big Yellow Taxi," Joni Mitchell penned the words, "You don't know what you've got 'til it's gone"—and she was right. Growing up as the big sister of a sibling with special needs has been the most rewarding experience of my life.
>
> But I would be lying if I said that I fully realized and appreciated it before my brother passed away. The light that others saw in Eric was finally revealed to me only after I had a moment to catch my breath and step out of the whirlwind that his arrival had caused twelve years prior.
>
> While Eric was alive, part of me saw him as a rude interruption of my perfect only-child status. Fortunately, I now realize he was so much more.
>
> Singer-songwriter Tracy Chapman wrote, "I've seen and met angels, wearing the disguise of ordinary people, living ordinary lives . . ." That was my brother.
>
> I believe Eric was placed into my world to teach me lessons about patience, love, and selflessness. He was so lovable and became absolutely delighted at life's smallest daily wonders. Looking back, there were so many things Eric taught me during his short time on earth. I am now genuinely grateful to have been blessed by his presence.
>
> Through the tough times and the fun times, it's the good memories—and Eric's laugh—that will stick with me forever.
>
> *I will always love you, little bro!*

SPECIAL TIPS

Caring for the siblings of your child with special needs means that you must be mindful of their needs and desires, too.

- *Make one-on-one time with the child without a disability a priority.* If that requires getting a sitter or respite care, do so. Siblings deserve your full attention, too. This kind of parenting effort can help your child make it through tough family moments, when special needs is especially demanding of your time and attention. Find time in your daily routine for alone time.

- *Encourage siblings to express their honest feelings about their role in the family.* Siblings may hold back powerful emotions to avoid adding stress to already stressed families or because they feel guilty about having negative feelings about their siblings. Let your children know that their feelings are normal—and it's OK to talk about and express them. Discuss some healthy ways they can release their feelings.

- *If despite your best efforts, your child has a hard time coping, seek professional help.* The special needs sibling role can challenge the most well-adjusted child and the best families. There is no shame in asking for help. Get past that limiting belief.

- *See your family's special challenges as a chance to model positive problem-solving for your children.* Children with brothers and sisters with special needs often display a maturity and sensitivity beyond their years, which can serve them well in other challenging situations. Help your children understand the important future benefits of their role.

- *Encourage your children to keep journals.* Then honor their privacy.

- *Don't be afraid to have more children.* "When you only have one child, parenting can become a narrow, intense relationship. There's not as much pressure with more kids," Sharon Emery says. "It's nice to have a parenting balance. What we gave our other children as a result of Jessica's needs is invaluable. I think they are who they are today because of her."

Special Resources

Here are a few resources that will provide you with additional information:

- Arthrogryposis: Virginia Simson Nelson, M.D., MPH, University of Michigan Dept. of Physical Medicine and Rehabilitation, 734-936-7200 or by e-mail: pedsrehab@umich.edu.

- Avenues: A National Support Group for Arthrogryposis Multiplex Congenita (AMC): http://www.sonnet.com/avenues.

- National Institute of Arthritis and Musculoskeletal and Skin Diseases: http://www.niams.nih.gov.

- National Organization for Rare Diseases, Inc.: www.rarediseases.org.

- National Rehabilitation Information Center: http://www.naric.com.

- Anxiety Disorders: Association of America: www.adaa.org.

- The Epilepsy Foundation: www.epilepsyfoundation.org.

- The Miracle League Ballfield: www.miracleleague.com.

- The National Center for Boundless Playgrounds: www.boundlessplaygrounds.org.

- USA Tech Guide to Wheelchair and Assistive Technology: links to wheelchair sports, recreation, and travel for kids, including horseback riding: www.usatechguide.org.

- David and Beth Frayer: frayerda@pilot.msu.edu.

- Sharon Emery and John Schneider: jschneider@lansing.gannett.com.

- The Sibling Support Project of the Arc of the United States/Sibshops: Don Meyer, director: 206-297-6368; www.thearc.org/siblingsupport; donmeyer@siblingsupport.org.

- *The Sibling Slam Book: What It's Really Like to Have a Brother or Sister with Special Needs*, edited by Donald Meyer, foreword by David Gallagher.

- *Views from Our Shoes: Growing up with a Brother or Sister with Special Needs*, edited by Donald Meyer, Cary Pillo, illustrator.

- *Living with a Brother or Sister with Special Needs: A Book for Sibs*, by Donald Meyer and Patricia Vadasy.

- *Sibshops: Workshops for Brothers and Sisters of Children with Special Needs*, by Donald Meyer and Patricia Vadasy.

- *How to Talk So Kids Will Listen and Listen So Kids Will Talk*, and *Siblings Without Rivalry*, by Adele Faber and Elaine Mazlish.

Special Note

Try hard not to abuse the use of siblings as caregivers. It's neither their role nor their responsibility—it's yours. If you are struggling with meeting the daily parenting demands of a child with special needs, seek out community resources designed to assist with such challenges. You have been given a wealth of such resources and links in this book. Access them!

Throughout *Breakthrough Parenting for Children with Special Needs*, you have been challenged to become a better child advocate by making more empowered parenting decisions—and by meeting the needs of all your children. Now let's honor two outstanding organizations that set the standard for special needs excellence—plus a young upstart that's coming on strong. Special Olympics and the Christopher Reeve Foundation (CRF) are special needs giants deserving of our kudos, and the Bubel/Aiken Foundation (BAF) is now aiming high . . .

PART FOUR

HONORING SPECIAL NEEDS EXCELLENCE

JUDY WINTER'S
SPECIAL NEEDS BILL OF RIGHTS
FOR PROFESSIONALS

You have the right to

- Be treated with dignity and respect
- Ask parents pertinent questions about their children's needs
- Ask for the training required to successfully meet the professional goals set for a child with special needs
- Advocate for necessary change within your profession
- Pursue honest and respectful communication with families
- Ask for professional support from your administration
- Ask that your time away from work be respected
- Request that homework be completed in a timely manner and that disruptive discipline issues be addressed
- Recognize a student's untapped potential and plan professional goals accordingly
- Understand that just because a child did not succeed with another professional, it does not mean that the child cannot succeed with you

10

HONORING SPECIAL NEEDS EXCELLENCE

Let me win. But if I cannot win, let me be brave in the attempt.
—Special Olympics Athlete Oath

As *Breakthrough Parenting for Children with Special Needs* comes to a close, I want to recognize some true champions, who shine the light on the value and potential of those with special needs on a worldwide stage: these are some of the heroes who continue to fuel my own work.

Special Olympics and the Christopher Reeve Foundation have helped foster priceless awareness of individuals of all ages with disabilities and have restored a sense of dignity to all those facing the daily challenges of special needs. And the Bubel/Aiken Foundation (BAF) is coming on strong.

I'm honored to pay tribute to all three in the final pages of *Breakthrough Parenting for Children with Special Needs*. I hope these tributes leave you inspired, energized, and ready to take on the world or, at the very least, your own school district.

We begin with one final success story about an award-winning, stand-up comedian with a hearing impairment. Kathy Buckley uses humor to showcase the power that one person holds to bring about change. Through laughter, this spunky, talented performer is challenging limiting perceptions about special needs—while living out her own big dreams.

SUCCESS STORY

Kathy Buckley is a great example of someone who has achieved impressive life success in light of living with severe hearing loss— and hitting a few giant potholes along life's rocky highway. The successful comic is often billed as America's First Hearing-Impaired Comedian, but her claim to fame runs much deeper.

Kathy Buckley is an actress, author, motivational speaker, and humanitarian, who also works as a consultant on special needs and job training for educators, corporations, and families—including coping skills for children.

Most of all, she is a survivor, and you won't believe *what* she's survived. Buckley was wrongly labeled as *mentally retarded* at birth. As a child, she was sent to a special education school, where it took the staff two years to uncover her hearing challenges. "And they called *me* slow," she jokes. Buckley speculates that a bout with infant spinal meningitis caused the severe hearing loss that kept her from speaking words early in life.

A school speech pathologist finally realized that the eight-year-old couldn't hear. For thirteen years, this skilled professional worked with the young child to facilitate speech— efforts Buckley credits with her ability to speak today.

Doctors warned Buckley's parents that she would be a slow learner and small in size. Instead she's six-feet tall and as quick as a whip.

Buckley was used to teachers thinking she was slow. She remembers a report card from second grade that stated she was "poor in using time profitably."

"Which we all know is the cornerstone of second grade," she responds dryly. "I always felt like a square peg in a round hole," Buckley says of her childhood.

Rather than talking about her disability, her parents gave her a hearing aid, a huge device that loudly distorted and amplified sounds that Buckley didn't want to hear, "like my mother's voice, and the annoying and loud *swish, swish, swish* of my corduroy pants rubbing together," she says. "It was enough to drive an eight-year-old insane."

When she refused to wear the contraption, her mother gave it away. "When she did that without discussing my disability with me, I thought that meant I was fixed. Instead I grew up not knowing who I was," Buckley says. "As a child, I didn't even know what my favorite color was. It was a very, very confusing time for me." She got by reading lips well.

Buckley's lack of disability support resulted in fear, frustration, and self-loathing, which took years to unravel and heal. For the first twenty years of her life, she contemplated suicide many times. Laughter became lifesaving. "Being funny was a protective mechanism," she says. "I got everyone to laugh first, so they wouldn't laugh at me."

In addition to her hearing loss, the comedian has survived child abuse, cervical cancer, living on food stamps, and rape. "I didn't know what sex was," she says. "I flunked sex-ed. They used animated filmstrips I couldn't lip-read!" She also spent two years as a wheelchair user after being run over by a lifeguard on an Ohio beach when she was a teenager. "I never heard her coming," Buckley now jokes. "I guess she didn't see my speed bumps."

It took five years of painful rehabilitation for Buckley to recover from her injuries. She was told she'd never walk again. "I didn't hear them say that," she quips. "So I just got up and walked away."

All this drama occurred before Buckley was thirty and is shared in her fascinating book, *If You Could Hear What I See: Triumph Over Tragedy Through Laughter*, which she cowrote with writer Lynette Padwa. "Between grammar and spell check, my computer lights up like a Christmas tree," says Buckley, who only recently learned to read, a result of her challenging childhood education.

After graduating from the Fashion Institute of Design and Merchandising (FIDM) in California, she struggled to find her voice. She credits a vocational counselor with helping her realize that her life had value.

Buckley was thirty-three years old when she finally realized that her learning struggles were the result of having a severe hearing impairment and not mental retardation—knowledge that helped change her life. "I stopped acting like a victim and took back my life," she says. She was finally ready to embrace her disability.

Today Buckley's life struggles are the meat of what she loves doing most—stand-up comedy at popular clubs like the Improv, Ice House, and Laugh Factory in Hollywood, where she has performed before capacity crowds. "In Hollywood, my disability is nothing compared to my being flat-chested and tall," she jokes.

Her stand-up career began on a dare in 1988, when she snatched away first prize from seasoned comedians. She judged audience reactions by floor vibrations, good acoustics, and skilled lipreading—something that doesn't work when she wants to enjoy the work of other top comedians, like Robin Williams. "His lips move too fast!"

Today a $4,000 state-of-the-art, computerized hearing aid allows her to hear the wild applause and the hecklers of sold-out houses. When a manager once told her she brought the house down, she responded, "I didn't touch anything!"

Buckley recalls the thrill of first hearing noisy crickets, the wind, talking to a parrot for hours, babies laughing, and birds singing. "It's not easy to lip-read a bird!"

Buckley received a *Los Angeles Times* Theater Ovation Award for Best Writing for her one-woman show *Don't Buck with Me/Now Hear This!* which debuted at New York's Lamb's Theater in 1999 to rave reviews, including from *The New York Times*. "I'm not deaf," she says in her act. "I just don't listen."

She also wrote and produced her PBS special "No Labels, No Limits!" (PBS Home Video, 2001), and has appeared on *The Tonight Show* with Jay Leno, *Good Morning America*, *Entertainment Tonight*, and *Touched by an Angel* and in *People* magazine.

Today Buckley is happily single. "I may be deaf, but I'm not dumb," she jokes. "There's something about a woman taking over a room of two thousand people that scares men," she adds. "They know if they mess up, they're my next bit." Buckley's future goals include having her own sitcom and appearing on *Oprah*. "But I don't think she can hear me!"

"Change your focus," she advises others who feel stuck. "Then get the heck out of your own way."

KATHY BUCKLEY'S TIPS

Life Success

From the vantage point of her incredible life experiences— and getting where she is now from where she was then— Kathy Buckley offers parents and children some great advice about how to realize their own big life dreams:

- *Remember that your child is a child first*. "Focus on what is there, not on what isn't. Focus on what that child needs. Everyone has something to contribute. Your children aren't broken; stop trying to fix them."

- *Believe in yourself*. "Never let someone else's ignorance keep you from reaching your dreams. If you have a dream, no matter how big, go for it!"

- *Surround yourself with positive people*. "Don't ever give away your power to other people to limit you," she says. "I've put a deaf ear to negativity!"

- *Enjoy your life*. Buckley says that in addition to love, the best thing parents can give their children is to enjoy their own life and be happy. "You are an example to your child. The ultimate gift you can give your child is the *gift of choice*—teach them to choose wisely."

- *Don't use disability as an excuse*. "My disability has not gotten me where I am today. How I have perceived it, used it, and laughed about it has. That's why I have succeeded," Buckley says. "I am so much bigger than my hearing loss. I am a human being *first*."

Kathy Buckley is proof that one person can achieve impressive success at any age, in spite of having special needs and facing tough circumstances—with the right attitude and hard work. Now let's recognize two outstanding organizations that have created greater special needs awareness worldwide.

THE GRANDDADDY OF THEM ALL— SPECIAL OLYMPICS

When it comes to organizations that work hard to improve the lives of children and adults with special needs, this one sets the bar of excellence.

With its unwavering commitment to "providing year-round sports training and athletic competition for children and adults with intellectual disabilities worldwide," Special Olympics inspires my own work. In the eyes of millions of families that enjoy its worldwide programs, Special Olympics is a special needs giant.

According to Kirsten Suto, in global public relations for Special Olympics, the program's athletes acquire valuable skills that also help them off the playing field. "We offer sports opportunities that build self-confidence, help athletes become part of the community, build friendships, and help them be accepted," she says. "We help others see that people with intellectual disabilities *do* have abilities."

Suto says that World Health Organization statistics indicate that 170 to 190 million people worldwide have intellectual disabilities, making it the world's single largest disability population.

It's hard to believe that Special Olympics is a grassroots effort that first began in 1962 as a summer day camp in Eunice Kennedy Shriver's backyard in Maryland, called Camp Shriver. Shriver is the founder and honorary chairperson of Special Olympics and executive vice president of the Joseph P. Kennedy, Jr. Foundation, which first created and funded Special Olympics.

"Eunice Kennedy Shriver opened her backyard and pool and allowed thirty-five people with intellectual disabilities to enjoy their summer in a setting where they could participate in sports and have fun," Suto explains. "In 1962, when many people with disabilities were still institutionalized, that was unheard of.

"Through her experiences growing up with her sister Rosemary, who had learning challenges, Mrs. Shriver knew that people with intellectual disabilities could participate in sports," Suto adds.

The camp idea caught on big in the United States and Canada, and in 1968, the first World Games were held at Chicago's Soldier Field. "That was when Special Olympics really began to bloom," Suto says.

Today two million athletes participate in more than two hundred Special Olympics programs in more than 150 countries. Athletes may choose from twenty-six different sports, including track and field, sailing, alpine skiing, snowboarding, tennis, swimming, cycling, softball, and volleyball. Participants must be at least eight years old and may exhibit a wide range of special needs, including wheelchair use. But a professional diagnosis of an intellectual disability must have been made before the child turns age eighteen. Participation is free to all athletes.

The athletes compete against like ability, gender, and age. "We are very different from other sports organization in this regard, including Paralympics," Suto says. "We like to say that participation in Special Olympics is about being your personal best, not THE best.

"We want people to understand that we are a year-round program that offers a variety of sports and volunteer opportunities in almost every community in the United States and throughout the world," Suto adds. "Special Olympics is for everyone."

A Conversation with Timothy P. Shriver, Ph.D.

When we spoke in June 2005, Tim Shriver was preparing to pass on his title as CEO and president of Special Olympics to Bruce Pasternack, so he could concentrate more fully on his role as chairman of Special Olympics.

Tim Shriver's love of Special Olympics first took root in his parents' Maryland backyard. From ages four to nine, the now chairman of the board of the global organization was immersed in the activities of the summer camp started by his mother, Eunice Kennedy Shriver, called Camp Shriver.

She began the summer camp to give individuals with intellectual disabilities the opportunity to experience recreational activities in a welcoming environment.

The special needs cause is also personal. Eunice Kennedy Shriver's sister Rosemary Kennedy had intellectual disabilities. She died on January 7, 2005, at age eighty-six. "Aunt Rosemary was a regular presence in our lives," Tim Shriver explains. "She was a strong inspiration to my mother. Whenever Aunt Rosemary visited, we would take long walks," he recalls. "She was a great swimmer and always involved in some recreational activity. Right up until her last visit, she was getting her bathing cap on."

Tim Shriver's family tree reads like a *Who's Who* of public service. His mother, Eunice Kennedy Shriver, started Special Olympics. His father, Sargent Shriver, was founder of the Peace Corps. His sister, Maria Shriver, is an author and the First Lady of California.

Tim Shriver graduated from Yale University. He has a master's degree in religion and religious studies from Catholic University and a doctorate in education from the University of Connecticut. He and his wife, Linda Potter, have five children. All have been involved in Special Olympics.

"They teach me that I can make a difference," he says. Shriver is an articulate, spirited, and compassionate man, whose indignation over the plight of millions of people with disabilities worldwide has fueled his work as chairman of the board of Special Olympics for nearly a decade. Shriver's passionate commitment to social justice—and his fire—remind me of his uncle Robert F. Kennedy, another of my heroes.

Tim Shriver's understanding of those with disabilities is deeply rooted in childhood. "I grew up in an environment where the introduction to special needs was in the context of play," he explains. "I didn't learn about this population in Sunday School or a service-learning class. I learned about them in my own backyard, when we had enough people, including several individuals with intellectual disabilities, for a kick-ball game or capture the flag or swimming events," Shriver says. "It was all about being exposed to same-age peers with whom we wanted to have fun. There was no pity, no guilt involved. It was fun to have kids over to play," he adds. "I think I was the luckiest kid in my neighborhood."

Tim Shriver embraces that concept of play today. "I consider that one of the great gifts of Special Olympics to this day," he says. "A lot of people think there is nothing they can do about injustice or that it will be painful or full of ugliness and pity. But you can encourage young people to get involved and help make a differ-ence—and have fun. There are very few things in life that are both important and fun." These powerful life lessons were learned at the feet of his parents.

"My parents combined an enormous energy to fight injustice," he explains. "That was never far from our dinner table discus-sions—that there were people in the world who were being denied a fair shake for whatever reason. There was injustice in the world," he says, "whether it was in Latin America or for African Americans in the United States or for those of different ethnic and religious groups—and it made them angry.

"It fueled a passion in them to make a difference, especially if the injustice was deliberate and not the result of unavoidable causes.

"Many of the lessons from my mother's childhood came from protecting Rosemary, making sure she was included, and reducing the amount of stigma and exclusion she might be experiencing," Shriver says. "But there is a broader issue here," he quickly adds. "My mother's work wasn't just about Rosemary. She discovered that Rosemary was one of tens of millions of people being discriminated against worldwide."

Tim Shriver says that in the early stages of Special Olympics, many athletes had been mistreated or were institutionalized. "So my parents created interventions designed to be fun. I've tried to do that in my own way," he adds. "My goal is to do things that I love, where I can add value.

"When most people hear the term *intellectual disabilities*, they think of people who can't dress themselves, can't make friends, can't understand movies—that they can't do anything. And we know that is just not true. This stubborn misunderstanding leads to widespread exclusion."

Addressing the underlying negative perceptions about disability is a strong focus of Tim Shriver's. In June 2005, he relinquished his titles as CEO and president to concentrate on his role as chairman of the board. "It will give me more of a chance to do more writing on this subject and to examine how the media can be more effective in their portrayal of individuals with disabilities."

Under Tim Shriver's capable leadership, Special Olympics began its Healthy Athlete Program and Athletic Leadership Program and political partnerships. "We involve political leaders in marshaling their energy that is drawn from their experiences in Special Olympics."

It was Shriver who set the goal of having two million athletes involved in Special Olympics by the end of 2005—a mission accomplished. But he's still not content. "That is still less than one percent of the world's population. We are still in our infancy regarding market penetration," he explains. "There are hundreds of millions of people who aren't involved in Special Olympics, who never get any kind of applause from a crowd of any kind.

"We still have lots of work to do running track meets, because that's what we do," he says. "But we also need to get much better at understanding what those events mean to people. People are hungering for the message that we can all get along, but they are afraid of people with disabilities," Shriver says. "When they come to our events, they find out they don't have to be afraid.

"It's all about acceptance and changing attitudes. We've got the market, we've got the message, and we've got the spokespersons. We just need to put it all together," he states. "We need to get this population out of the pity, condescension category into the empowerment category." That empowerment includes addressing educational inclusion.

"Right idea—long way to go," the former teacher says of inclusion. "There is not enough responsibility placed on kids without disabilities to make inclusion work. Real inclusion works at the level of peer groups," he explains. "We need to challenge young people to define their schools as places of inclusion."

"Be proud of your sons or daughters," Shriver tells families. "They are fantastic human beings who have a huge array of gifts and the potential of lighting up the lives of hundreds of thousands of people."

 DID YOU KNOW?

Eunice Kennedy Shriver may just be the ultimate special needs sibling. Because of her experiences growing up with her sister Rosemary (who had intellectual disabilities and had passed away in 2005), the founder and honorary chairperson of Special Olympics and vice president of the Joseph P. Kennedy, Jr. Foundation knew that people with intellectual disabilities could participate in sports—and strongly believed they deserved that opportunity.

Shriver helped give birth to Special Olympics and gave athletes with intellectual disabilities opportunities to realize their dreams of successfully participating in year-round sports training and competition—and in life.

The mission that first took root in 1962, in Eunice Kennedy Shriver's backyard, has grown into an international special needs giant.

At the historic first World Games, held in Chicago in 1968, Eunice Kennedy Shriver said: "I have new heroes and they are the parents of persons with intellectual disabilities. They demanded that their children be treated like other children.

(*continued on next page*)

(continued from previous page)

They said, 'My children are of value.' In ten or fifteen years, we are going to have millions of athletes in Special Olympics around the world and the parents are going to say to everybody, 'We won.'"

On March 24, 1984, President Reagan awarded Eunice Kennedy Shriver the Presidential Medal of Freedom, the nation's highest civilian award, for her work on behalf of people with intellectual disabilities.

Today she continues to travel internationally to accomplish in other countries what she has helped achieve in the United States. "We have opened doors in the world, and that is all inspired by Eunice Kennedy Shriver," says Kirsten Suto, in global public relations for Special Olympics. "Mrs. Shriver is a true pioneer."

For more information on the work of Eunice Kennedy Shriver and Special Olympics, visit http://www. specialolympics.org.

TURNING TRAGEDY INTO TRIUMPH— THE CHRISTOPHER REEVE FOUNDATION

With the exception of Special Olympics, no one has done more to elevate the dignity and awareness of those with special needs than Christopher Reeve, while driving home this reality: *disability can happen to anyone at anytime*.

I remember first hearing of Christopher Reeve's horseback-riding accident in May 1995—a seemingly inexplicable event that left the skilled stage actor, film star, and horseman a quadriplegic, unable to move his arms and legs or breathe on his own.

Although many people bemoaned the end of Superman's physical abilities and leading-man status and questioned his future, I remember thinking that perhaps the special needs cause had just gained a powerful new voice and advocate. I had no idea how high he would raise the bar for the rest of us.

Christopher Reeve brought increased awareness of people with special needs to a whole new level, including in the political arena—where he became a respected, powerful force and made critical political inroads. He commanded important doors open before wheeling through them with dignity, intelligence, charm, passion, and conviction—and yes, that Hollywood smile. This superman ended up fueling hope for millions.

Maggie Goldberg is vice president of public relations for what is now the Christopher Reeve Foundation (CRF). She shares some key facts about spinal cord injuries (SCI) and the ongoing work of the foundation. "CRF is committed to funding research that develops treatments and cures for paralysis caused by SCI and other central nervous system disorders, including spina bifida, multiple sclerosis, and ALS," Goldberg explains. "The second part of our mission includes working vigorously to improve the quality of life for people living with disabilities." It's a big focus of CRF board chairperson, Dana Reeve.

Goldberg says between 250,000 and 400,000 Americans live with paralysis as the result of spinal cord injuries (SCI). Of these, 82 percent are male; 55 percent of the injuries occur between the ages of sixteen and thirty. "As we work to broaden our mission, we know there are four million Americans living with paralysis as the result of any mobility impairment."

The foundation first began as the Stifel Family Paralysis Foundation, funded by the family of Henry G. Stifel III, who had a spinal cord injury. "At that time, spinal cord injury research was considered the graveyard of neurological research," Goldberg says.

In 1982, this foundation merged with the American Paralysis Association (APA). "When Christopher Reeve was injured in May 1995, he was impressed with the way the APA was operating," Goldberg says. "So in 1996, he joined the board as chairman and created the Christopher Reeve Foundation. The two organizations officially merged in 1999 and became the Christopher Reeve Paralysis Foundation (CRPF).

"The merger didn't change the way we funded research or the fact that Christopher Reeve was the spokesperson," Goldberg explains. Reeve's name automatically increased the awareness of spinal cord injury and the budget quadrupled. Additional funding went to research and quality of life grants. In 2005, the foundation returned to its roots and the original name of the Christopher Reeve Foundation (CRF), with a new motto: Go forward!—words spoken by Christopher Reeve months before he died when asked by reporters what advice he gives others living with spinal cord injuries.

Goldberg highlights two current key efforts of the Christopher Reeve Foundation:

• *The Christopher and Dana Reeve Paralysis Resource Center (PRC)*. Goldberg says the PRC is fully funded by the federal government and is the nation's clearinghouse for people living with paralysis. "Those recently injured or those living with paralysis for a long time can e-mail or call us for support." The PRC was created to establish a single, focused national resource on paralysis and addresses such topics as travel, health, tools and technology, research, rehabilitation, insurance, employment, benefits, materials for children, and active living. "We are very proud of this three-year-old program." The PRC also publishes an extensive print manual: *The Paralysis Resource Guide*. For more information, contact the PRC at www.paralysis.org, e-mail: prc@crpf.org, or call 1-800-539-7309.

• *Christopher Reeve Foundation Superman Tags*. "Warner Brothers has graciously offered us use of the Superman logo for three years, beginning in 2005," Goldberg says. Tags are available on their Web site as dog-tag necklaces or clips. All money raised goes to supporting the Christopher Reeve Foundation.

A Conversation with Dana Reeve

Dana Reeve, chairperson of the board of directors of the Christopher Reeve Foundation, lovingly stood by her husband after his accident and continues his mission to find a cure for spinal cord injuries. Reeve is committed to improving the quality of life for families facing disability, including through the Dana and Christopher Reeve Paralysis Resource Center (PRC).

When we spoke in June 2005, Dana Reeve talked about her husband's legacy—and about the future of the Christopher Reeve Foundation (CRF). Shortly after this interview, Dana Reeve was diagnosed with lung cancer and was undergoing chemotherapy.

Christopher Reeve is often equated with Superman. And his wife Dana is no slouch either. The forty-three-year-old chairperson of the CRF is an accomplished actress and singer, who has starred on Broadway and appeared on such television programs as *Law and Order* and *All My Children*. She is the author of CAREPACK-AGES: *Letters to Christopher Reeve from Strangers and Other Friends*.

But Reeve says she is first and foremost a dedicated mom to son Will, now thirteen, and stepmom to "two terrific adult children, Matthew and Alexandra."

"Will is doing great," Reeve says. "He is an amazing kid, who has the strength and focus of his dad. He's a gentle young man, a wonderful athlete and very resilient. I'm lucky to have him."

Dana Reeve believes a child's gifts are the direct result of how a parent approaches life adversity. "Chris and I believed that you can choose to dwell on problems or solutions," she says. "We always tried to dwell on solutions. We discovered that you can have joy and laughter within pain and hardship and you can still make a difference."

When Christopher Reeve died on October 10, 2004, the world mourned the loss of this special needs advocacy giant. For the family, the loss runs much deeper.

"I miss Chris all the time, and sometimes more acutely than others. But we are *going forward*, which is what Chris always wanted for us. He left such important work behind, and it feels great to be able to carry that on." She says that the grief has eased somewhat. "But then it curls back on itself and is as fresh as ever."

After Chris died, Dana Reeve spent a whirlwind year answering media requests and working hard to ensure that her husband's groundbreaking work for paralysis lives on.

The Christopher Reeve Foundation and the Christopher and Dana Reeve Paralysis Resource Center are committed to funding medical research to find a cure for paralysis, while also providing grants to programs that help improve the quality of life for those living with a wide range of paralysis, including spinal cord injury, cerebral palsy, spina bifida, and multiple sclerosis. Changes are in the works.

Today the work of the foundation addresses a broad spectrum of need. "When Chris was injured, he focused on a cure for spinal cord injury," Reeve says. "But as he lived with his injury and we became well versed in what it's like to live with disability in this country, his focus really broadened."

The PRC arm of the foundation is funded by the Centers for Disease Control (CDC) and addresses paralysis of any cause, while also funding nonscientific quality-of-life grants. "We address the day-to-day quality-of-life issues for those living with paralysis," Reeve says. "For example, we funds lots of camps for kids with disabilities."

The foundation is also active in caregiver-respite legislation, a bill that keeps getting stalled. "We are asking for government-subsidized funding," she says. "Family caregivers relieve such a burden off the system, for very little return. Families do it out of love, duty, and devotion. But they shouldn't be penalized for having those qualities."

Reeve also feels strongly about the controversy over stem cell research. Only 10 percent of CRF funding goes to this research. "We do so many programs for those with disabilities, but stem cells get in the news," she says.

"Stem cell research is controversial, so that's newsworthy. Ironically, this was unlikely to be the most beneficial treatment for Chris. But we continued the work because part of our belief system has always been valuing biomedical research and improving the quality of life for every human being." She wishes her husband could have witnessed the May 2005 passage of the Stem Cell Research Enhancement Act by the House and Senate. "He worked so hard at that. That was a poignant moment for me—and a fight I want to finish for him."

Reeve believes there will be a cure for paralysis in her lifetime. "The *aha!* moment would be if clinical trials started to be substantially successful in humans," she says. "The work they are doing in the labs is evidence that it can be done. But there are roadblocks."

Like many special needs advocates, Christopher Reeve became frustrated by the politics involved in creating important and necessary change for those with disabilities.

"Chris was always involved politically, even prior to his injury. He was a political animal, so it was a natural place for him to go. He always had success with his political lobbying in the past, but this was different. It was very difficult to make inroads. Chris saw the money there; he saw the need; and he saw the big roadblocks. It was extremely frustrating for him."

Dana Reeve believes the growth of the foundation is her husband's greatest life contribution. "We very quickly became not just a family foundation but a prominent not-for-profit and an internationally known foundation. We are also considered a model for other foundations and now have a Washington office," she explains.

"For Chris to bring the foundation to such a place of stature and effectiveness and live the life he did and be the husband he was and the dad he was is just amazing," Reeve says. "It was a huge accomplishment."

Reeve also feels strongly about educational inclusion. "I feel like it should be mandatory," she says. "It raises awareness and sensitivity in such positive ways to have kids with disabilities in the classroom," she says. "Our friends have told us that they see it as such a blessing that their children have grown up with our family because the experience has been so character building and so enriching."

On the day we spoke, Dana Reeve was at her summer home in the Berkshires, a cultural haven and family escape in Massachusetts, where she was taking time to reflect on the loss of her husband and then her mother, to ovarian cancer, both in the same year.

"Chris and I met here when we were both performing at the Williamstown Theater. We got married here and Will was born here. This is a particularly grounding and creative place for me," she says.

"Chris had such impact on the world and personally on my life. He was a person who lived life with deep meaning and purpose. He is still a very powerful presence in my life."

Dana Reeve laughs when asked if she ever thought of her husband as Superman. "The Superman identity has been imposed by the public," she says. "Chris was an actor. It was one of the roles he played and people responded to it because he did such a great job. Part of the reason he played the part so well is because he was a person of strength, integrity, and sensitivity, the combined qualities of Clark Kent and Superman.

"Basically, everything Chris did he did well, so when faced with this disability, he had the fortitude and determination to take this incredibly challenging experience and turn it around and do good for others," Reeve explains. "It was typical of his personality to achieve things in life at the highest level. In that sense, the term *Superman* is symbolically powerful."

During the nine and a half years that Christopher Reeve lived with a spinal cord injury, his wife never wavered in her commitment to him—honoring the true meaning of the vows *for better or worse*. "I don't really believe in the destiny of one person being meant for another person," she says. "But I do believe in graceful intervention and knowing when something is right and worth working for."

She says of her life with her husband, "We were a tremendous partnership and it was a wonderful love affair."

She has strong words for those who argue against what they call *false hope*. "What a ridiculous thing to pick on. Why would you do that? Why would you take the one thing that is keeping someone going and pick it apart?" she asks. "People would say to Chris, 'You are lobbying for funding that engenders false hope,' and he would say to them, 'There is no such thing as false hope. There either is hope or there is not.'"

Dana Reeve is grateful that her husband chose to live with hope after his accident, when he could have implemented a do-not-resuscitate order to end his life. "When he came back into consciousness, he said that maybe we should make the decision to let him go," she says. "I told him, it's your life and your decision, but you should know that you are still you and I love you and I am in it for the long haul.

"I've been thinking a lot about that decision lately, and all I feel is gratitude," Dana Reeve says. "I'm grateful Chris had the strength and courage to make the decision to live and for the nine and a half years we had as a result. I would not be the person I am today without those years, nor would my son."

DANA REEVE'S TIPS

Caregivers

Dana Reeve has walked the special needs walk well. Her valuable advice comes from the heart.

- *Get as much support as you can.* Reeve believes strongly in this. She suggests accessing the National Family Caregiver's Association, which she says is great in terms of providing support, networking, and literature. Visit www.nfcacares.org.

- *Use all the resources at your disposal.* "The Christopher and Dana Reeve Paralysis Resource Center is a great place to go because it's free! It's a resource that is already there for you. I always found that any kind of reaching out always made me feel better," she says. "Talking to someone who can help you come up with an answer is priceless." Visit www.paralysis.org.

THE NEW KID ON THE SPECIAL NEEDS BLOCK: THE BUBEL/AIKEN FOUNDATION

As this book goes to press, there is no doubt that Clay Aiken is one of the best-selling *American Idol* contestants of all time. But it's what this idol has done with his fame that most impresses me—and the reason I'm recognizing him as *one to watch* in the future of special needs excellence.

Aiken is a graduate of the University of North Carolina, with a degree in special education. He is also chairman and cofounder of the Bubel/Aiken Foundation (BAF).

The foundation's mission includes working toward societal inclusion for all children with special needs, especially those with autism. Aiken's partner in the creation of BAF is its executive director, Diane Bubel, the mother of a child with autism named Michael, who is Clay Aiken's friend. We first learned about this special partnership in Chapter Two's Success Story. The BAF slogan is Opening Doors: Opening Minds. Aiken was also appointed as a national UNICEF ambassador in 2004. I predict that this talented, enthusiastic young teacher will continue to be an agent for positive change for children with special needs for years to come, including through the work of BAF. Thanks, Clay Aiken, for *all* that you do to help create important change for this deserving population!

 DID YOU KNOW?

According to information on her official Web site, Marlee Matlin was only twenty-one years old when she became the youngest recipient to ever receive a Best Actress Oscar for the film *Children of a Lesser God,* her film debut. To learn more about the impressive life achievements of this award-winning actress and mother, who is deaf, visit www.marleematl insite.com. Check it out!

THE FUTURE OF SPECIAL NEEDS

When I first began this journey, I carried a huge sense of responsibility for making positive changes for families with special needs. As I see how many people have now taken up the cause, I realize my load is not as heavy as it once was. I am filled with hope for the future of our children.

Our society is no longer as clueless about disability, and I feel like I can finally take a deep breath and let it all out.

When this book took root in 1990, it was born partly of the seeds of my anger and outrage, mixed with a whole lot of love. I was on a mission to improve my son's life—and the lives of other children. *Breakthrough Parenting for Children with Special Needs: Raising the Bar of Expectations* is the realization of my dream years ago to help families walk this path a bit easier than those who had walked it before them, including me. I hope that in some small way, I have accomplished that mission.

Fact is, there has never been a better time to have a child with special needs, which should leave you feeling increasingly hopeful. But don't be fooled into thinking that this parenting highway is now paved with golden ease.

We continue to face serious funding concerns and legal challenges, plus the enormous need for quality, affordable services for families breaking under the weight of their demands. That includes the crucial need for respite and family support services and better insurance coverage. The issue of inclusive education is still a hot bed of discussion and not yet guaranteed. Our work is far from over.

Still, I strongly believe that all these challenges can be met through the sheer determination and sweat of millions who care about this population. Don't you dare get complacent! One person *does* hold the power to have an impact and make big changes.

Breakthrough Parenting for Children with Special Needs is filled with their examples. *I* didn't know that when I first started down this rocky road, but because of this book, now *you* do.

Use that knowledge well. Then add your own experiences, with a dash of wisdom, spunkiness, and a great deal of humor to keep the special needs advocacy flame burning brightly. We *cannot* let the momentum burn out!

My son's daily needs no longer spur me on, but I will always be deeply committed to actions that improve the lives of children and families with special needs. My parenting role has now changed, so I am passing the daily parenting torch on to you.

But I will be walking alongside you.

Now roll up your sleeves and get busy, because a child with special needs is counting on you—and I'm going to be watching you closely.

Do us all proud . . . !

 DID YOU KNOW?

Throughout *Breakthrough Parenting for Children with Special Needs: Raising the Bar of Expectations,* I have challenged you to become better child advocates. So for our readers who are United States citizens, here's the contact information for the White House. Don't forget to contact your friends in the House and Senate, too. Readers in other countries can contact their own key policymakers and decision makers.

Now please go write an intelligent, well-supported, passionate letter about an important special needs issue directly affecting your family. Let your voice be heard in Washington. And take your advocacy to a whole new level!

The White House Web Site is http://www.whitehouse.gov. Contact information for the White House is http://www.white house.gov/contact/.

FirstGov.gov is the official U.S. Web site for all government information, services, and resources. DisabilityInfo.gov is the online resource for Americans with disabilities.

SPECIAL TIPS

Special Tips concludes by repeating what I believe to be the single most important parenting tip you can embrace. It underlies everything you do to support a child with special needs. *This belief will make you fearless!*

Believe in Your Child's Value—No Matter What!!

Special Resources

Here are a few resources that will provide you with helpful information regarding topics addressed in this chapter:

Organizations

- The Bubel/Aiken Foundation (BAF): www.thebubelaiken foundation.com.
- Clay Aiken's official Web site: http://www.clayaiken.com.
- United States Fund for UNICEF: www.unicefusa.org.
- The Christopher Reeve Foundation: http://www.christopher reeve.org.
- The Paralysis Resource Center: www.paralysis.org.
- Special Olympics: www.specialolympics.org; info@ specialolympics.org.
- American Association on Mental Retardation (AAMR): www.aamr.org.
- The Joseph P. Kennedy, Jr. Foundation: www.jpkf.org.
- Kathy Buckley: www.KathyBuckley.com; contact@kathy buckley.com.
- Alexander Graham Bell Association for the Deaf and Hard of Hearing: www.agbell.org.
- American Speech-Language-Hearing Association: www.asha.org.
- House Ear Institute: Advancing Hearing Science:

www.hei.org.

- National Association of the Deaf (NAD): www.nad.org.
- National Institute on Deafness and Other Communication Disorders (NIDCD): www.nidcd.nih.gov.
- The National Theater of the Deaf: www.NTD.org.

Books

- *Your Child's Hearing Loss: What Parents Need to Know*, by Debby Waldman and Jackson Roush.
- *Living Well with Hearing Loss: A Guide for the Hearing-Impaired and Their Families*, by Debbie Huning.
- *Living with Brain Injury: A Guide for Families*, by Richard C. Senelick and Karla Dougherty.
- *What's Wrong with Timmy?* by Maria Shriver.
- *Enabled in Words: The Real Lives, Real Victories of People with Disabilities*, by Keith Landry, Sarah Lopez, and Yudha Pratama: www.enabledonline.com.
- *Still Me* and *Nothing Is Impossible: Reflections on a New Life*, by Christopher Reeve.
- *No Excuses: The True Story of a Congenital Amputee Who Became a Champion in Wrestling and in Life*, by Kyle Maynard.

Special Needs Excellence Honorable Mention

In addition to all the terrific people and organizations already included in *Breakthrough Parenting for Children with Special Needs*, here are just a few of those individuals whose important work continues to further the cause of children with challenges. *Thank You!*

Individuals and Organizations

- Christopher Burke: *Life Goes On;* Down Syndrome (DS); spokesperson for the National Down Syndrome Society. The official Chris Burke Web site: www.welcome.to/chrisburke. Book: *A Special Kind of Hero*.

- Cher: www.Cher.com; national chairperson of Children's Craniofacial Association: www.ccakids.com; Keep a Child Alive (HIV/AIDS): www.keepachildalive.org.

- Michael J. Fox: *Family Ties;* Parkinson's disease. The Michael J. Fox Foundation for Parkinson's Research: www.michaelj fox.org; book: *Lucky Man: A Memoir*.

- Jerry Lewis: Jerry's Kids for Muscular Dystrophy (MD); Jerry Lewis MDA Labor Day Telethon; official site: www.mdausa.org/telethon/.

- Marlee Matlin: deafness/hearing impairment; Marlee Matlin official Web site: www.marleematlinsite.com; book: *Deaf Child Crossing*.

- Fred (Mr.) Rogers: http://pbskids.org/rogers; founder and CEO of Family Communications, Inc.: http://www.fci.org.

- Marlo Thomas: national outreach director for St. Jude Children's Research Hospital (founded by her father, Danny Thomas): www.stjude.org; books/CDs: *Free to Be . . . You and Me, The Right Words at the Right Time,* and *Thanks and Giving: All Year Long*.

- Oprah Winfrey: the *Oprah Winfrey Show; O, the Oprah Magazine;* and *the Angel Network:* www.oprah.com.

Television

These are some of the shows that have created positive awareness of those with special needs by regularly writing, casting, and portraying this population with honesty, sensitivity, and dignity. Most of these programs have aired in prime time.

- ABC: *Life Goes On; Once and Again; Extreme Makeover: Home Edition*
- CBS: *Touched by an Angel; Joan of Arcadia*
- NBC: *ER; Hallmark Hall of Fame*
- PBS: *Mister Rogers' Neighborhood; Sesame Street*

Special Note

I have shared with you many of my own parenting experiences—now I'd like to hear about yours! Please write and tell me how *Breakthrough Parenting for Children with Special Needs: Raising the Bar of Expectations* has affected your life. And share your success stories with me! Your words may be included in future revisions or for additional projects for *Breakthrough Parenting for Children with Special Needs*.

Write me at jappwinter@aol.com (no attachments, please!), and be sure to visit my Web site for future updates: www.JudyWinter.com. Or write me at P.O. Box 454, Dewitt, Michigan 48820.

Thank you for the incredible honor of accompanying you on this *amazing* parenting journey! By working together, we *are* changing the lives of families with special needs—and granting priceless gifts to our children.

I will forever cherish the amazing blessing and privilege of *always* being Eric's mom. I hope that you, too, experience the very best that special needs parenting has to offer. I look forward to reading your heartfelt words.

In the meantime, I wish you *Godspeed*—and a good night's sleep . . .

ABOUT THE AUTHOR

Judy Winter is an award-winning newspaper, magazine, and online journalist and columnist. She parented a musically talented child with cerebral palsy for more than a decade, until Eric passed away in February 2003. Her rich and vast experiences as a parent, journalist, and advocate for special needs have provided her with the knowledge, compassion, and wisdom she now shares in the pages of *Breakthrough Parenting for Children with Special Needs: Raising the Bar of Expectations*.

The author's work also appears in the books *A Special Kind of Love: For Those Who Love Children with Special Needs* and *Enabled in Words: The Real Lives, Real Victories of People with Disabilities*.

Judy Winter is recipient of the Michigan Federated Chapters of the Council for Exceptional Children 2002 Exceptional Parent Award. Her work as a columnist has been recognized in Distinguished Achievement Awards for Excellence in Educational Reporting from the Association of Educational Publishers.

She is included in the Twenty-Fifth Silver Anniversary (2006–2007) edition of *Who's Who of American Women*, honoring excellence in professional achievement.

Judy Winter is cochair of the annual Eric 'RicStar' Winter Music Therapy Summer Camp at Michigan State University and a former board member of United Cerebral Palsy (UCP) Michigan.

The author resides in Michigan with her husband, Dick, where they love escaping to Northern Michigan, especially Mackinac Island. Their daughter, Jenna, recently received her bachelor of arts degree in visual journalism from Brooks Institute of Photography in California.

Judy Winter brings passion to all she undertakes.

INDEX